Dedication

This book is dedicated to our Lord who invited my wife Carol and me on a "walk with the Father" that we might know Him. It was on that walk with Him in Myanmar and the days of studies in the Word that the greatest love story ever told became clear to us. He has been faithful to His words that *"if you seek Me with all of your heart you will find Me"*. His Word continues to become clearer and more beautiful each day as His nature and His love for His people is constantly being revealed. Throughout all time He has written/is writing the greatest love story of longsuffering, redemption, and of oneness with Jesus Christ (King of kings) and the Father. For this reason we bow our knees in awe of His nature and His greatness. We need not imagine this love story, for this very day in our time we are the actors in this; the greatest of love stories ever told. Experiencing Him as we walk with Him.

All things are from Him, through Him, and to Him
For His Kingdom according to His will

Emray Goossen

Table of Contents

Preface

We all enjoy a good story teller as we imagine the places and the actors described in the story. If it is a good story, if it is told well, we begin to put ourselves into the story by imagining ourselves as the main character. We see the stage. We see the set on the stage. We envision the house, the land, and the country as told by the storyteller. As we relate with the struggles, the pain, and the joy of the actor through our imaginations, we vicariously experience the life of the actor through the storyteller.

Consider for example this short story.

Just 35 years old Nicolas was already an experienced traveler and explorer. He loved to visit other lands and cultures. But he was pretty set in his ways as he thought he had pretty much seen everything. He was in full control of his life and did what he wanted as seemed right to him.

He had come with three other friends to this far off land to explore the culture and its beliefs. There were so many crazy ways different cultures expressed their existence and rules of life. But he was certain there was but one life and he had made up his mind to live it as he wished according to his desires.

As they traveled this land they came to a high mountain. The road was so steep and so long that the car overheated on the climb up the 30° slope. But Nicolas had learned patience and did not let the delay stress him out for the expectation of the discoveries waiting for him at the top of the mountain. When they reached the top they were greeted by the coolness of the altitude, a welcome escape from the tropical temperatures below.

It was evening by the time they had found their room and checked in. So after a short meal they took a walk to the west side of the mountain to watch the sun set. There they spotted a border to another kingdom they did not expect. There were military emplacements on the tops of every high mountain and hill overseeing the border to protect it from illegal entry. Nicolas had not known that this kingdom existed. Being a traveler and explorer his curiosity was raised.

There were a number of other people standing there watching the sunset. Standing a bit apart from the tourists Nicolas saw some individuals whose clothing indicated they were locals from different tribes, each wearing the garb representative of their unique heritage. But there was one who stood alone wearing something unique, an elegant royal type of cloak. So Nicolas went up to this man and introduced himself. The man identified himself as Samuel.

Nicolas pointed to the far away hills on the other side of the border and asked Samuel if he knew anything about that kingdom. Samuel responded; "I am a citizen of that kingdom". Excitedly Nicolas began to ask Samuel question after question about that kingdom. What were the people like? What was the foundation of their economy? What kinds of grains, fruits, and vegetables were grown there? Samuel reached into his bag and pulled out a fruit and gave it to Nicolas. This is one of the fruits grown in my kingdom he explained – taste it. Nicolas peeled the skin and took a bite from the juicy meat of the fruit below. His taste buds exploded with new flavors he had never experienced before. The fruit was refreshing, tasty, and filling all at the same time. Nicolas had never tasted anything like it. Samuel explained that this fruit was grown only in the kingdom and was being exported to other lands by the citizens of the kingdom as they temporarily lived in those lands. The king had sent them out to do just that; share the fruit of the kingdom with those who had never tasted of it and to discover those who might be interested in becoming citizens of the kingdom.

The sun had set so everyone departed to their own places. Nicolas went to his room with his three friends and tried to explain what he had heard and how the fruit tasted but he saw he just could not get his friends to grasp what he had experienced. That night Nicolas could hardly sleep as he pondered on what that kingdom and the king was like. He tried to devise a plan how he might visit that kingdom but he was unable because he knew absolutely nothing of it. So his sleep was fitful at best.

The next morning he rushed through his breakfast and ran off looking for Samuel but could not find him. By midafternoon he was worn out and discouraged in his search so he sat down under a large banyan tree. He was startled when he heard a voice off to his left, commenting about the nice day. He had been staring at the ground caught up deep in his own thoughts. He looked up and to his surprise the man was wearing the same type of clothing as the man Samuel had been wearing the night before. The man warmly introduced himself as David.

Oh, Nicolas exclaimed; "are you from that kingdom over there?" It did not take long for Nicolas to get to his point; "where do I go to get into the kingdom so that I might see it and visit with its citizens?" But David gave Nicolas some bad news. The kingdom is closed to visitors and tourists. Only its citizens can enter.

Shocked because he had never been turned away from his desires, Nicolas wondered to himself if he might enter the kingdom illegally. But as he pondered this David explained the impossibility of entering the kingdom except through one door, the one place which the king provides. There is no qualification that anyone from another land can achieve in order to obtain a visa. No amount of money, no purchase price is sufficient to buy a visa from the king. Only those who know the king and who the king knows will be granted a visa. So Nicolas asked; "how then can one become known by the king?"

For the rest of the afternoon and that evening David explained the king and the kingdom to Nicolas. How the king had created the kingdom. How his people had been led into rebellion by a deceiver only to enslave them. But then how the king had purchased the citizens from slavery and invited them into His kingdom at great cost to himself. He was not a conquering king by force as are other kingdoms on earth. He paid the purchase price of slavery to set the people free and is inviting them into his kingdom by their own choice.

As Nicolas left to go to bed he heard David speaking to someone. He turned and looked. David was speaking as though through some communication device. Nicolas could not hear a response to David's words but he heard David mention his name and ask something for him.

The next morning David came to meet with Nicolas at breakfast. He asked Nicolas many questions about his desires to enter the kingdom. He spent some time explaining again who the King was and His nature.

Finally David asked Nicolas if he was interested in becoming a citizen of the kingdom. Would Nicolas trust this king and give his allegiance to Him? By this time Nicolas was convinced and so wanted to enter this kingdom. So David told Nicolas to call the king. "Call the king how", Nicolas asked. David explained that the king can hear you speak. So Nicolas followed David's prompting to call the king, humbly asking to be granted entry into the kingdom. To Nicolas joy he found that right there and then, immediately, he was given a passport seal that identified him as a citizen of the kingdom. Guaranteeing his citizenship for all time.

That is a story that hopefully engages your imagination. A story that causes you to visualize the view from the top of the mountain and to relate to the main actor Nicolas. It would fit within the genre of fantasy novels except that it is a parable of sorts that illustrates elements of the greatest love story ever told of the King of kings and the kingdom of God. You might not be aware of the existence of the kingdom of God as Nicolas was. The only idea or evidence that it exists is going to come from those who have visited there, the citizens of that kingdom. The only evidence you might get of its nature is through the fruit the citizens export and the stories they tell as did Samuel and David. If you get to that point you will be given the news that there is only one door into the kingdom and that the qualifications for entry are beyond any human ability. However, if you continue to seek you will find that the King has provided the free qualifications for entry himself. But the cost to you is high; you must surrender to the King and deny yourself. Yet the price of entry is a free gift from the King to anyone who would choose Him. This is the greatest love story of all time that we will explore through the words of the King Himself.

It is a great love story for which we don't need to use our imagination. We don't need to imagine this story, because this story is real. This story was real in the past, is real now, and will continue into the future. We don't have to imagine ourselves as one of the actors in this story because we are the actors in this story. Today you and I are living out our part in the greatest love story ever told of the King of kings. What we see, what we feel, and the decisions we make are all part of the story. It is not an imaginary play. We are living in the real love story of the King of the ages.

The following pages will explore the nature of the King, His kingdom, and His people. Hopefully you will find some inspiration that you as an ambassador of the kingdom can use to invite the Nicolas in your life into the kingdom of God.

The purpose of this book is to open our eyes to the story of the King and His love for His people.

- **To grasp the reality of this great love story, and our presence within the story.**
- **Most importantly for us to know the King through His nature and His love story.**
- **To understand the kingdom of God that we might teach the Gospel of the kingdom rightly**
- **To be encouraged as laborers in a vineyard to go and teach its citizens the wealth of the treasure they have in the King so that they might realize the joy of exporting the fruit of the Kingdom to all the world.**

**For His Kingdom according to His will

Introduction

This book was inspired through a study of the Gospel of John. Early in the Gospel of John we read about a conversation between a ruler of the Jews, Nicodemus and Jesus Christ. In this conversation Jesus highlights the importance of understanding the Kingdom of God.

There had been much controversy within the Jews regarding Jesus. Many Pharisees wanted to kill him. They saw Jesus had healed the sick on the Sabbath and in so doing He had broken the law given through Moses to do no work on the Sabbath. So they considered Jesus a common sinner. Yet Jesus had shown authority over creation and taught in a way that no prophet before Him had done. One evening a Pharisee, a man named Nicodemus a teacher of the Law, came to Jesus when it was dark so that no one could see him. Jesus, as always, switched the conversation to the spiritual need of the person He interacted with. In this case Jesus told Nicodemus *"unless one is born again, he cannot see the kingdom of God"* (John 3:3). These words took Nicodemus by surprise.

Here Jesus introduced two new topics not heard of before;

1) You must be born again, and
2) The Kingdom of God

The possibility of entering the kingdom of God draws us. We don't know what it is like but we imagine it is a beautiful orderly place as it must be the place where God dwells and rules. We expect that it would be a place of peace. It would be a privilege to enter this kingdom. So, the idea of the existence of a kingdom of God that a man could possibly enter made Nicodemus listen. Jesus, however, put a stipulation on entering the kingdom of God. You must be born again.

It seems that if there is a place we want to go we should understand a bit about it before we buy a ticket to enter that land. Well, the Bible does a pretty good job describing the kingdom of God, what it is like, where it is located, and when it will be established. Interestingly the phrase "kingdom of God" or "kingdom of Heaven" is not used in the Old Testament but appears 207 times in the New Testament.

It should be sufficient cause for us to pursue understanding the kingdom of God when we read that Jesus said *"I must preach the kingdom of God"*, ***"for this purpose I have been sent"*** (Luke 4:43). This purpose is just as significant as His statement *"for the Son of Man has come to seek and to save that which was lost"* (Luke 19:10).

Jesus demonstrated this importance by sending His disciples out for the purpose of preaching the kingdom of God (Luke 9:1-2).

Not only did Jesus demonstrate the importance of preaching the kingdom of God by sending out His disciples to preach the kingdom of God. We also find how important the kingdom of God was to Jesus when He focused on *"speaking of the things pertaining to the kingdom of God"* with the disciples during the 40 days after His resurrection (Acts 1:3).

If the Son of God came to Earth for a primary purpose of preaching the kingdom of God we should take note!

If Jesus gave this charge to His disciples that they should preach the kingdom of God would Jesus then not also expect us to preach the kingdom of God as well. We see that the early church preached the kingdom of God along with preaching the name of Jesus Christ.

> *But when they believed Philip as **he preached the things concerning the kingdom of God and the name of Jesus Christ**, both men and women were baptized (Acts 8:12).*

If we are expected to preach the Gospel of the kingdom of God then should we not understand the kingdom of God?

So we raise some questions:

1) When is the kingdom established?
   - Is it when Jesus rules the earth for 1000 years?
   - Is it after Jesus 1000 year reign?
   - Does the kingdom exist today?

2) Where is the kingdom of God?
   - Is it on the earth?
   - Does it reside in heaven?
3) What makes up the kingdom of God?
   - Is it a physical kingdom?
     or
   - Is it a spiritual kingdom?

We generally think of kingdoms in physical terms where the boundaries between kingdoms are visible. So we are likely to define the kingdom of God in a physical sense. **Biased by our desires we may think of the kingdom of God as a place in which we can live instead of the place in which the King lives.** We often think of this kingdom as a place in which, in some future time, we will live happily ever after relaxing and just enjoying the food the King provides for us each day. We remember the story of that beautiful place the King made for the first two citizens, Adam and Eve, and may think that is what the kingdom of God will be like. But the kingdom of God is not found in any of these places.

We can learn much about a kingdom by studying the character, nature, and interests of a king. So to begin with we need to understand a little bit about the King of the kingdom.

The King of the kingdom of God is not an ordinary citizen of the kingdom who has been chosen by His subjects to rule, neither has He taken control of the kingdom by force. The King is much greater than the citizens of the kingdom. The King was not born, defining the beginning of His life. He has no beginning. There is no day that says He is one year older. There is also no end to His life. The King is the source of life itself.

Those who have not entered His kingdom do not know or understand that it is only through the King one may enter into His Kingdom. They do not understand that words of truth come only from this King. All other words come from the father of lies, the destroyer of the relationship between the King and His people.

1   Preparation for the Kingdom

Even though the phrase "kingdom of God" is not spoken in the Old Testament, the history recorded in its pages reveals, as though veiled, the King's plans to restore His people to Himself in this great love story.

This great love story began a long time ago when the Father and the Son (our King), the center of this story, made everything. He created time itself. It was through Him that all the worlds, all the seas, all the mountains, all the trees, and all the animals were made. But the King not only made the land, He made the subjects of the land. It was through Him that people were made in the image of the Father, Son, and Spirit (The Triune God). Made with a soul, with a body, and with a spirit. He created Adam and Eve, the father and mother of us all. He placed our first grandparents, Adam and Eve, in a beautiful garden with all kinds of fruits to eat and everything they needed to live. The King came to the garden every day to walk and talk with them. It was a place of peace and joy without death. So Adam and Eve began their life completely innocent, not knowing good and evil.

The problem in this story began in the very garden created by the King. The King has an enemy, the Great Dragon, Satan, a thief, the father of lies, and a murderer. He came to steal the kingdom from the King. To this day he is working to deceive us and steal our souls from the King. His lies to Adam and Eve created doubt about the truthfulness and character of the King. He told them that they could be like the king, ruling themselves. Unfortunately Adam and Eve desired the fruit and the "power" offered to them by the Great Dragon. Acceptance and pursuit of these lies began the rebellion against the King which is still going on today.

Adam and Eve realized good and evil and felt shame the moment they disobeyed the King and ate of the tree of knowledge of good and evil. They tried to cover their shame by sowing together leaves to cover their nakedness, a symbol of the many futile efforts that man has done through the ages to pay for his sins. But at the very beginning the King demonstrated the cost of their rebellion with the blood shed by an animal to provide skins to cover their shame. And through that initial act the King showed man that though he was unable to cover his shame, the King would provide.

In this act the King demonstrated that the penalty for their sin of rebellion was death. Life giving blood had to be shed. Then in the nature of His love the King provided a substitute, likely a lamb, which had to die, shed its blood, and give its skin to cover their shame. Already, from the very beginning, the King was illustrating His plan to save His people and bring them back to Himself. Already the King was demonstrating his great love that carries throughout the greatest love story ever told.

When the King cast Adam and Eve out of the garden it was not for punishment, it was for love. Lest they would eat of the tree of life and live for eternity in with an evil nature. He cast them out that they might receive the gift of life in repentance from sin. That they might become righteous and holy through what the King would accomplish. This was for love in from the beginning.

There was a judgement, a penalty for sin. Through their sin death entered the world. But even in judgement the King exhibited His love. As the King pronounced His individual judgment on the serpent (Satan), on Adam, and on Eve he spoke of a Seed, a descendant, who would defeat the destroyer. Today we know Him as our Savior, the King Himself, who would come 4,000 years later to rescue the children of men for all time. In the beginning He promised that this Savior would crush the head of the enemy, the deceiver, the Great Dragon, Satan. It was the King who would pay the price of death, shed His blood for the cost of repayment of the debt of rebellion and sin. Mankind needed the King to intervene, and so He did.

Adam and Eve had children. Their children had children. Generation after generation until today. Now it is you and me. We are all of the same family, we are descendants of Adam and Eve, the first people created by the King. Because we are their children and because the enemy planted rebellion in the hearts of our ancestors we are all born with the nature to doubt the King and the desire to be our own ruler. Because of this we do evil things. Because of this we carry a debt for our rebellion. A debt to great for us to pay. We need a permanent, a lasting payment, and we need to be changed.

History shows us that most of the people before us, just like us, did not want Him as their King. They continued to want to rule their own lives as their own king, not knowing that in so doing they made the deceiver their king. It is recorded that there were some who desired to serve the Creator King but all of them were just unable to keep the laws of the kingdom on their own power. They were unable to live up to the perfection necessary to restore a clean and pure relationship with the holy King. Not one man throughout history has been able to live a life pure enough to pay his debt of rebellion before the King. Not one man could make enough sacrifices or earn enough merit sufficient to remove the shame and pay the debt he owed to the King because of his own sin. All along the way man's desire to rule himself turned to worshiping trees, the sun, and other parts of the Kings creation. Man worshiped the very things he carved out of wood and stone in order to serve his own desires and wants. In effect the deceit of Satan ruled, as man ultimately served himself as his own god.

Key actors and their behaviors are recorded in the Old Testament history that we might see the longsuffering of the King in this great love story. Longsuffering in his mercy and love to mankind who could never measure up to the holiness and righteousness of the King on their own merits. Longsuffering in his mercy and love as the King exercised justice and correction on those who He loved.

The King never forgot His people or the children of their children. They could not see Him as He is but there were some that walked with Him in their thoughts, their minds, and their deeds. From them we have great historical records of how the King continually revealed Himself throughout history as though through a veil. These short stories of their lives present a picture that the King was painting in this love story through time of what He was going to do to save His people and bring His people back to Himself.

Job who was called a righteous man by the King in speaking with Satan, had difficulty in submitting to the King. Yet the King blessed Job greatly after his trials.

Abraham, with whom the King made a covenant of land and many descendants, and who is considered the father of faith, did not believe the King and so fathered a child with Sarah's maid servant when the promised child had not yet come. Abraham did not trust the King when he lived as if his wife Sarah was his sister. Yet the King did give Abraham a son, Isaac, by his wife Sarah. Later the King tested Abraham's faith by asking Abraham to sacrifice his son. Again the King provided a vision of the King's future substitute payment for man's sins by providing a substitute ram for Abraham to sacrifice. The promise of many descendants was by the faith in the King to which Abraham testified. It is through Jesus Christ, the King, the many descendants promised to Abraham have come, descendants who are of the faith.

Moses who is considered the father of the Law was prevented from entering the Promised Land because of a rebellious moment. Yet the King used Moses mightily in rescuing the descendants of Abraham, the Children of Israel, from slavery. There was none like Moses who spoke face to face with the King. It was through Moses that the plagues were put upon the Egyptians that convinced them to let the Children of Israel go. Moses was the one through whom the King gave the instructions for escape from the angel of death that was to slay all the firstborn of the land. The slain lamb, the blood on the door posts, and the Passover of the death angel again provide an illustration of the coming Lamb of God who would provide an escape from death to those who believe. It was also through Moses that the criteria for righteousness before the King was written down in the 10 commandments. A standard of righteousness that man cannot keep on his own power. Laws like; you shall not kill, you shall not steal, you shall not want your neighbor's wife. It was the first law that they should have no other gods than the King, their Creator that was the most difficult law to keep because of their desire to be the rulers of their own life.

Along with the Law the King sent prophets. Prophets to teach the people the ways of the law so that they might keep them. They acted as guides and disciplinarians as they gave direction and provided correction. But the people treated these prophets poorly, beating some and killing others. The people could not, did not want to overcome their desires to be their own ruler, continuing to live in doubt of the Creator King.

This is the nature of man since the enemy came and put doubt and the desire to rule into his heart. Today you and I are living in this story with the same struggle. Each person is tempted by his own desires to rule over his own life and to serve himself making gods of stone and wood, gods of business, and gods of beauty to serve himself. Unwittingly in so doing we serve the enemy, Satan, the father of the rebellion.

The law and the prophets have shown us the true nature of what the children of Adam and Eve are like without their King. They/we have no hope outside the King. No matter how much man struggles to keep the law man will always fail. No one has been found pure and holy throughout time, no prophet, no priest, and no monk. No sacrifice has been found that can pay the debt for the sin of rebellion. There are not enough self-inflicted punishments, not enough offerings, not enough self-denial, not enough merits a person can do to pay for his debt. Man remains hopeless in his own meager righteousness before the holy righteousness of the King.

But there is hope. It is found only in the King Himself.

Here the story line takes a dramatic change. It was the King who made the payment for man's rebellion. The King stepped into His own creation coming in the form of a man. He was born in the womb of a Virgin, Mary, a descendent from Adam. But the King was not conceived in the flesh. He was conceived in the womb by the Holy Spirit (Matt 1:20). Although

He came in the likeness of man's sinful flesh (Rom 8:3) or the form of a man He was still the Creator, the Son of God without sin. We know Him as Jesus Christ. As He walked the earth he demonstrated His authority and identity as the King. King over creation by commanding the winds and the waves. King over health as He made the blind see and lame to walk. King over life and death as He raised the dead to life. King over all spirits and demons who obeyed His commands and identified Him as the Holy One of God. Then God the Father identified Him audibly as His beloved Son.

The King gave His own life as the pure spotless Lamb of God to be crucified on a cross for the debts of rebellion and sin for ALL peoples. The sacrifice of the Lamb of God is symbolically illustrated throughout history. Through His death He paid the debt no one could pay. Through His resurrection he gave eternal life to those who believe on Him. He made the sacrifice once for all; for all sins, past, present, future. He set free from the debt of sin all who would believe on Him. Those who would accept the purchase and surrender to Him as King. The purchase price of His rebellious people, His own blood.

That was His plan from the beginning. Where Satan had placed doubt, He offered trust. Where Satan had placed desire for self-rule and death, the King offered life in surrender to the rule of the King of kings. Where man's rebellion and separation from the King brought death, the King brought life. Where man did not know love, He gave love. The payment and the freedom from the debt of rebellion are the work of the King. He made it very simple; accept Him as our Lord and trust in His work, trust in His love. The King is life and through accepting Him as King we have eternal life.

Because of this change in the storyline we who believe and put our trust in the King are no longer under the law and the prophets. We gain entry into the Kingdom of God to be with Him by accepting the purchase of our souls by the King's own sacrifice, the door He opened for us. With the debt paid by the King Himself all the decedents of Adam and Eve are granted the choice to serve Him as King and Lord, or not. It was and is each one's decision to enter the Kingdom or not.

So the king is sending out the call and invitation to enter the Kingdom to all the descendants of His people, every tribe and every nation. Every individual, every person. He did not come as a conquering King but as a King who purchased our hearts at the cross with the price of His life, because of His love. For those who choose Him He comes and lives in the place He purchased, our hearts, which then becomes the place of His Kingdom. A kingdom where the King rules and his will is done.

The building of His Kingdom is continuing today. You and I are in this story. We are not watching a play or imagining a story. We are living in the story, part of the story. Our choices and our actions tell the story of our lives in the bigger story of the King.

1.1 The Law

Before Jesus (the King) came to earth to teach the Kingdom of God He gave the Law. The standards of purity necessary for mankind to live by, by which they might walk with the King. The King sent Prophets as teachers to the people to instruct them in understanding and obedience in accordance to the Law, and to call for their repentance to live righteously. Looking back we now know that the King used this time under the Law as a teacher, a tutor, to demonstrate man's inability to keep the Law. From the beginning the King knew man could not keep the law or make sufficient sacrifice to pay for his rebellion and so He would come as the promised Savior.

1.1.1 The Law given

It was 1,450 years before Christ that the Law was given to Moses in Sinai.

When the children of Israel escaped from slavery in Egypt they had camped at the base of a mountain named Sinai. It was there that God first gave His law. Simple instructions on how a man might live a righteous life before God. Here God spoke to Moses saying:

"I am the Lord your God, who brought you out of the Land of Egypt" (Exodus 20:2–17)

1. You shall have no other gods before Me
2. You shall not make for yourself a carved image....
3. You shall not take the name of the Lord your God in vain....
4. Remember the Sabbath day, to keep it holy, six days you shall labor and do your work...
5. Honor your father and mother...
6. You shall not murder
7. You shall not commit adultery
8. You shall not steal
9. You shall not bear false witness against your neighbor
10. You shall not covet your neighbors...house...wife... servant...anything that is your neighbors

1.1.2 The Purpose of the Law

The law gave the criteria, or standard, according to which a man must live for holiness before a holy God. These requirements of the Law demand behavioral requirements that can only be held by a pure and holy heart. The condition of the heart that man is unable to change through any activity or discipline by his own power.

History has demonstrated that not one man has been able to keep all the law. Not one priest, not one prophet, not one holy man could ever keep all the law. *"All have sinned and fall short of the glory of God"* (Rom 3:23). Everyone is guilty of turning away from the one true God. All of mankind's efforts towards righteousness have been and are futile and hopeless. All the sacrifices, all the meditations, all the self-denials are an insufficient sacrifice for the sins of any man. So the law demonstrates mankind's inability to be holy before God. *"If there had been a law given which could have given life, truly righteousness would have been by the law"* (Gal 3:21). If there was just one law given that gave life that man could keep then the efforts to keep the law would have resulted in holiness before God.

In the weaknesses of not being able to keep the law and not being able to make sufficient sacrifice everyone's need for God's mercy is demonstrated. All mankind is *"confined all under sin, that the promise by faith in Jesus Christ might be given to those who believe"* (Gal 3:22). The only way to God is through the provision from the Father; the Son of God, Jesus Christ. The only hope comes through the King of kings.

So then the law was, *"our tutor to bring us to Christ the King, that we might be justified by faith"* (Gal 3:24). The law showed us our evil nature and our need for the Creator Himself to provide an escape from sin that we might receive forgiveness from sin. But now as we have accepted *"by faith"* that which the law pointed us towards, Jesus Christ our Savior, *we are no longer under a tutor"* (Gal 3:25). The law, our tutor, brings us to understand our need for the King to rescue us. Through our faith in the King we are no longer under the Law, tutor, whose purpose was to bring us to the King.

All the religions of the world, except for Christianity, are based upon the works of keeping the law of their religion. Even some Christian denominations and churches add their own rules and call them laws of God. They impose them on their believers as behaviors they must keep in order to be holy before God. Many religions make images of stone and wood and then worship them. In so doing they *"worship and serve the creature rather than the Creator"* (Rom 1:25). They make much of prayers and sacrifices to these gods of stone. They follow their own laws which can never make them perfect.

The sacrifices of man must be continually given over and over again because there is no sacrifice that is enough. And then man's nature insures that he will sin again. The sacrifices of man are never finished. The examples of the children of Israel makes this clear. They offered sacrifices for their sins continually for the laws they broke. But all their sacrifices could not make them perfect otherwise *"would they not have ceased to be offered"* (Heb 10:1–2).

So the Law was given as a preparation for the coming kingdom of God, demonstrating man's futility in being like god in attaining holiness by his own efforts. As a tutor the law points man away from the deceit of doubt towards the King and the desire of being one's own king and ruler of his own life. In executing the continual sacrifice for his sin the Law demonstrates man is unable to live a holy life and is unable to atone for his sin unto holiness.

1.2   The Prophets

The King also gave His people prophets, prophets to teach and admonish the people about God's Law and to expose their sins unto repentance. These prophets did not speak on their own but were men through whom God spoke to His people. God's chosen vessels through whom He communicated to the children of Israel. They would often petition God for advice on such things as who would be the next king and whether or not to go into battle. Most often we read that the prophets were calling for the children of Israel to repent or God would send judgement upon them.

From the time of Moses until the last judge, Samuel, God provided judges who administered judgment of the law on the children of Israel.

The first prophet of the Old Testament is Elijah who lived 870 years before Christ. Elijah did not die but was caught up into heaven *"a chariot of fire appeared with horses of fire, and separated the two of them; and Elijah went up by a whirlwind into heaven"* (2 Kings 2:11). Elijah was therefore considered by the Children of Israel as a principle prophet representing all the prophets. So much so that the Children of Israel were looking for Elijah's return as a sign of the arrival of the Messiah. To this day when they celebrate the death angel Passover in Egypt as a remembrance of what God had done, part of their ceremony is looking for Elijah's return.

1.2.1 Prophetic actions

There were many works and activities done by the prophets of the Old Testament. To tell them all would take weeks. These few are but a very small sampling of the work done by Elijah:

- Elijah prayed that it would not rain for 3 years because of the sins of king Ahab. It did not rain for 3 years. After three years the Lord spoke to Elijah saying to present himself to Ahab and I will send rain. (1 Ki 17:1, 1 Ki 18:1)
- Elijah lived with a widow woman and her son who only had a handful of flour and a little oil. The flour and oil never ran out. There was always enough to eat. (1 Ki 17:12-16)
- The widow's son became so sick he died. Elijah prayed to the Lord and the son was restored to health. (1 Ki 17:17-24)
- Elijah spoke the word of God to king Ahab. These were words of judgement and king Ahab did not like Elijah's continual messages of judgement from God. (1 Ki 18:17-18)
- Elijah had king Ahab arrange for a challenge between God and the god Baal. So 450 prophets of the god Baal pleaded all day long, dancing and cutting themselves as they begged their god to send fire on the altar of Baal. Elijah mocked them saying that maybe their god was asleep or on vacation. So they pleaded and cut themselves all the more. At evening Elijah had them pour much water on the altar and the sacrifice that he had built to God. Then he prayed only once and fire came from heaven, burned up the sacrifice, burned up the rocks of the altar, and consumed all the water in the ditch around the altar. (1 Ki 18:19-40)

1.2.2 Purpose of the Prophets

The purpose of a prophet is found in how he is described. These short phrases speak of the way in which God gifted a prophet to do His work:

1. a man of God (1 Kings 12:22), meaning that he was chosen by God
2. a servant of the Lord (1 Kings 14:18), indicating that he was to be faithful to God

3. a messenger of the Lord (Isa. 42:19), showing that he was sent by God to carry a message
4. a seer, or beholder (Isa. 30:9–10), revealing that his insight was from God
5. a man of the Spirit (Hos. 9:7; Mic. 3:8), indicating that he spoke by the Spirit of God
6. a watchman (Ezek. 3:7), a man on alert for God
7. a prophet, a spokesman for God

Through the prophets God demonstrated His authority and His power. Through the prophets God taught the people His statues and His Laws. Through the prophets God admonished the people regarding their sins. Through the prophets God foretold of things to come.

In summary, all of the prophetic titles refer essentially to the same function, that of a man receiving a revelation from God and relating it to others. They were ambassadors of God bringing a message and the word of God to the people.

1.3   Transfiguration Signpost

In the King's story through time He placed certain events that delineated changes in the way He dealt with man. We are all aware of the flood, the tower of Babel, Abraham, and the law given after God rescues the Children of Israel. We also remember the birth, death, and resurrection of Jesus Christ.

But there is a very important change that takes place when Jesus comes to walk the earth. We understand that Jesus is the fulfillment of the law and prophets because He said *"do not think that I came to destroy the Law or the Prophets. I did not come to destroy but to fulfill"* (Matt 5:17). But have we recognized the signpost that God gave to illuminate this fulfillment?

There is a switch, a change in the message of the storyline from God that took place at that event. It was the revelation of the King, Jesus, the spotless Lamb of God. The veiled plan of the King's restoration of His people was fully revealed.

The law and the prophets were preached until John, but since that time John the Baptist and Jesus began preaching the Kingdom of God (Luke 16:16). Not even the disciples grasped the significance of this signpost until later. But God gave us a visual illustration of the change in focus from the Law and Prophets to His Son in this signpost in the storyline of His great love story.

Two men represent the law and prophets. Moses was the recipient and deliverer of the law. Elijah was the first of the prophets after the judges were replaced by kings. Both men held the respect of these roles as God's representatives. Moses is the representative of the Law and Elijah is the representative of the prophets. This signpost brought Elijah and Moses together standing on the mountain when Jesus was transfigured. With Peter, James, and John as witnesses the Father speaks; *"This is My beloved Son, in whom I am well pleased. Hear Him!* (Matt 17:5).

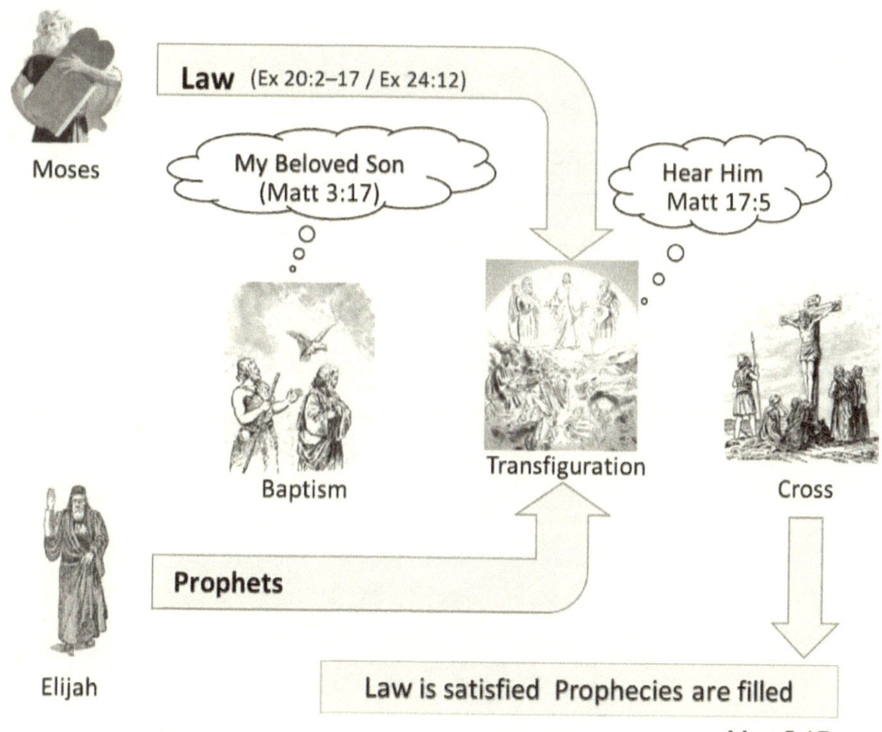

Transition Signpost of God

From the time of Moses God had given the law for man to keep. From the time of Elijah God had given prophets to watch over the people and admonish them with the words of God to keep them on the path of righteousness. The children of Israel were to keep the law given by Moses and the words of God spoken by Elijah and the prophets. But man could neither keep the law nor make sacrifices sufficient for their sins.

This delineation in God's story and timeline separates the way in which God deals with man. He has now provided a Savior, His own Son, as man could not save himself. God transitions the focus from the law and the prophets, teaching man his helplessness, to Jesus the Savior. All three; Jesus, Moses, and Elijah were standing together. It is a coming together of the law and the prophets into one, Jesus. A transition to Jesus, who now solely carries the Words of God.

God placed this signpost in time when he assembled the representative of the Law (Moses), and the representative of the Prophets (Elijah) on the mount with the King of kings Jesus. Jesus had said that until John the Baptist the Law and Prophets were preached. But now the Kingdom of God is preached. Then on the mount with Moses and Elijah standing beside Jesus, God the Father speaks and says *"This is My beloved Son, hear Him"*. The Father closes the chapter in time of following the Law and Prophets and opens up the chapter in time for mankind to listen to the Words of His Son Jesus Christ. Now hear Him!

Don't miss this signpost!

2   The King of the Kingdom

Any study of a kingdom must include an understanding of its king. We can learn much about the kingdom of God as we; hear from the King, observe the King's behaviors, and hear what others say about the King. For it is the King who is building the Kingdom of God. So we must spend some time here to proclaim the King; Jesus Christ the Son of God, the Creator, and the King of the Kingdom of God.

We look for some criteria that identifies the king:
- What is the lineage of a king?
- What/who identifies him as king?
- Is he able to demonstrate he has authority over his kingdom?

In the four Gospels we find these proofs that Jesus is the only Son of God, the Messiah, and the King through:
- His genealogy or family line
- His demonstrated authority over that which He created; the winds and water, physical healings, authority over spirits and demons, and life and death
- Fulfilled prophecies about Jesus as the Messiah
- The testimonies of; apostles, soldiers, John the Baptist, the Father, Jesus Himself, and the witness of many men
- Jesus own resurrection and ascension

We would expect that the King of the kingdom of God would be able to demonstrate His authority. From Jesus walk here on the earth we see the testimony of; His works, His authority over all things, all other gods, all spirits, the eye witness accounts to His authority, and God the Father Himself declaring Jesus as the Lord and King.

2.1   Genealogy of the King

The Word tells us that Jesus is both God and Man. He is the only begotten Son of God who came in the form of a Man to provide the perfect sacrifice for man's sins. The Bible records Jesus lineage through:

- The parents of his "supposed" earthly father Joseph – all the way back to Abraham
- The parents of his earthly mother Mary – all the way back to Adam
- Jesus lineage to His Father as the only begotten Son of God, begotten by the Spirit in the womb of Mary

2.1.1   Jesus: as Man

Let us first look at Jesus the man through the line of His "supposed" earthly father. Jesus was thought to be *"(as was supposed) the son of Joseph"* (Luke 3:23). Jesus was supposed to be the son of Joseph because Joseph was the husband of Mary. Unless it was known that Jesus was conceived of the Holy Spirit in Mary when they were betrothed and had not yet known each other the people and the disciples would have believed Jesus to be the son of Joseph. So Joseph was but Jesus legal father through whom His lineage is traced back to Abraham. Whereas the natural physical ancestry to mankind is traced through His mother Mary.

The lineage of Jesus through His "supposed" father begins with *"Abraham begot Isaac, Isaac begot Jacob, and Jacob begot Judah and his brothers"* (Matt 1:2) and finishes with *"And Jacob begot Joseph the husband of Mary, of whom was born Jesus who is called Christ. So all the generations from Abraham to David are fourteen generations, from David until the captivity in Babylon are fourteen generations, and from the captivity in Babylon until the Christ are fourteen generations." (Matt 1:16-17).*

This is the line of Jesus through Joseph his father – BUT Joseph is his father in name only, not his biological father. Joseph represents the "legal" ancestors of Jesus through the "man" as if Joseph was his physical father.

Now let's turn to Jesus earthly mother Mary. At the end of Mary's list of ancestors we find the first man Adam, so Mary's line is traced all the way back to the first man *"the son of Enosh, the son of Seth, the son of Adam, the son of God" (Luke 3:38)* Adam. Through His mother, Mary, to God's creation of the first man Adam we are given the physical lineage of Jesus. Notice that Adam is called a son of God – he is a created son, not a natural born son.

Now it was thought that Jesus was the son of Joseph, but He was not. Jesus earthly body was conceived of by the Holy Spirit. For this clarification we have to go back to the birth announcement of Jesus and how Mary became pregnant.

Mary, a virgin, was betrothed to a man named Joseph who was a descendant from King David. She was not yet married and had not known a man. The angel Gabriel was sent by God to tell Mary that she would have a child. Of course Mary questioned this saying *"How can this be, since I do not know a man?" And the angel answered and said to her, "The Holy Spirit will come upon you, and the power of the Highest will overshadow you; therefore, also, that Holy One who is to be born will be called the Son of God* (Luke 1:34-35). Gabriel told her that the Holy Spirit would come upon her. The power of the Spirit of the One who is over all things and creatures would come over her and she would conceive a son who is the Son of God.

The angel Gabriel also told Mary that she should call her son Jesus and that God would give Jesus the throne that was promised to His ancestor David when he was king of Israel. That Jesus would be called the Son of the Highest. This is not a natural conception as of a man and a woman who through relations with each other would conceive a child. Jesus was the Son of God Himself who came in the form of a man, born in the likeness of a man (Phil 2:5-8). The same one who was at the beginning and created all things.

2.1.2   Jesus: as God

Now we consider Jesus as God. In the very beginning it is recorded that God said *"let Us make man in Our image"* (Gen 1:26). The words "Us" and "Our" are not singular. Furthermore the word used in Gen 1:26

"Elohim" is a plural word in Hebrew. That "Us" refers to The Father, The Son, and The Holy Spirit.

These three are all God. The Father is not the Son nor the Holy Spirit and yet the Father is God (1 Cor 8:6). The Son is not the Father and not the Holy Spirit and yet is God (Heb 1:8). The Holy Spirit is not the Father nor the Son and yet is God (Acts 5:3-4). God is three and yet God is One (1 Jo 5:7).

God is One Deut 6:4, 1 John 5:6-8

That Jesus was God at the beginning of Creation is told to us in the Gospel of John *"In the beginning was the Word, and the Word was with God, and the Word was God. He was in the beginning with God. All things were made through Him, and without Him nothing was made that was made"* (John 1:1-3). The *"Word"* being identified as Jesus who became flesh and lived among us (John 1:14). The Word who was the only begotten One of the Father, the Son of God (John 3:16).

So we see Jesus is the only begotten Son of God. We see that all Creation was made through Jesus. He was at the beginning with God and yet Jesus is God.

This claim that Jesus is God was made by Jesus Himself. Jesus appeared to Moses as the "Angel of the Lord" at the burning bush and identified Himself as YAHWEH the "*I AM*" (Ex 3:13-15). The "I AM" who has no beginning and no end, before time, He is self-existent.

It was during a discussion with the Scribes and Pharisees that Jesus states clearly that He is the "I AM". They had just gone through an argument about who Jesus was, questioning His ancestry with the Jews claiming that they were descendants of the revered Abraham. They thought they had caught Jesus in their trap when Jesus told them that anyone who kept His word would never taste death. Ah they said; the prophets are dead and Abraham is dead, so who do you make yourself out to be? Then Jesus tells them that Abraham rejoiced to see His (Jesus) day. So how was this possible, Jesus was less than 50 years old and Abraham lived long ago? How could you, Jesus, have seen Abraham? Jesus makes this telling statement *"Most assuredly, I say to you, before Abraham was, I AM"* (John 8:58). Jesus claims that He is the "I AM", God Himself.

It was also God the Father who declared *"This is My beloved Son, in whom I am well pleased* (Matt 3:17). It was the Father who declared Jesus as His Son and as God (Heb 1:8).

2.1.3 Jesus: God and Man

Jesus was born of the Virgin Mary, conceived by the Holy Spirit. He humbled Himself and came in the likeness of men and the appearance of man. *"Christ Jesus, who, being in the form of God, did not consider it robbery to be equal with God, but made Himself of no reputation, taking the form of a bondservant, and <u>coming in the likeness of men</u>. And being* *found <u>in appearance as a man</u>, He humbled Himself and became obedient to the point of death, even the death of the cross"* (Phil 2:5-8).

He did not give up his divinity in coming as a child born of Man. He came in the form and appearance of a man but He was still God. So He was born without the sin of Adam, in effect He was a new creation, a new Adam. *"...There is a natural body, and there is a spiritual body. ⁴⁵ And so it is written, "The <u>first man Adam became a living being</u>." The <u>last Adam became a life-giving spirit</u>. However, the spiritual is not first, but the natural, and afterward the spiritual The first man was of the earth, made of dust; <u>the second Man is the Lord from heaven</u>"*. (1 Cor 15:44-47). This speaks of a comparison between Adam and Jesus. Adam became a created living being but Jesus came as the Lord from heaven a life-giving spirit in the form of a man. Adam was the natural man taken from the dust of the earth, the Creation. Jesus was spiritual in the form of man the Lord from heaven. Jesus took on the form of a man but He was/is God.

2.1.4   King of Kings and Lord of Lords

The words of prophecy tell us Jesus position will be revealed as the King of Kings and Lord of Lords at the end of time.

> *Now I saw heaven opened, and behold, a white horse. And He who sat on him was called **Faithful** and **True**, and in righteousness He judges and makes war. His eyes were like a flame of fire, and on His head were many crowns. He had a name written that no one knew except Himself. He was clothed with a robe dipped in blood, and **His name is called The Word of God.** And the armies in heaven, clothed in fine linen, white and clean, followed Him on white horses. Now out of His mouth goes a sharp sword, that with it He should strike the nations. And He Himself will rule them with a rod of iron. He Himself treads the winepress of the fierceness and wrath of Almighty God. And He has on His robe and on His thigh a name written:* **KING OF KINGS AND LORD OF LORDS** *(Rev 19:11–16).*

He will be revealed in all power and authority. He will wear a crown and His name will be revealed as the **Word of God** which we also saw in John 1:14. He is a righteous judge and returns as a conqueror who makes war as commander of the armies of heaven. He will then rule with a rod of iron. As a judge He executes the punishments crushing those who do not follow Him. Throughout time the King had held out His hands to His people to invite them to come back to Him. Then He gave Himself to pay the debt of their rebellion. But at the end of time He will be in full glory and authority executing judgement on those who refuse His gift of love.

2.2   Authority of the King

There is a large body of evidence that Jesus Christ is; God, the Creator, the only begotten Son of God, and our Savior. The works or miracles he did demonstrated that He as God as the King; has authority over all creation, has authority over all spirits, has authority over death and life, and is the coming King of the Kingdom of God. The Word is filled with this evidence and testimony. We will only touch on just a few samples of them here covering the categories of proofs that Jesus is who He said He is.

2.2.1   Authority over creation

One of the proofs that Jesus is who he claimed to be is His authority over Creation. It is written that at the time of creation He spoke and created all things (Gen 1:3-26). If He is the Creator then He will be able to speak and command that which He created to do His will. This He did. He demonstrated this many times and in many ways. During his time on earth he turned water into wine (John 2:1-11), commanded the winds and waves (Mat 8:23–27, Mark 4:35-41), filled the fishermen's nets with fish (Luke 5:1–9, John 21:5–6), fed thousands essentially from nothing and walked on water (Matt 14:13–33, Matt 15:32–39).

In the passage of (Matt 14:13-21) Jesus traveled up to the Sea of Galilee as He had a number of times during His ministry. There on the shore of the Sea He taught the people and healed the sick all day long. Towards evening time the disciples had become concerned about the people becoming hungry. It was here that Jesus fed 5,000 men (not including women and children) from five loaves and two fishes. Not only was Jesus healing the sick all day, not only was Jesus teaching the Word of God all day, he then fed 5,000 from five loaves and two fishes. Then to make the testimony complete each disciple (12 of them) picked up a basket full of food as an individual testimony to each of them. He had the power to multiply food with just a prayer of blessing to His Father.

This demonstrates Jesus power over creation as He multiplies these five loaves and two fishes to feed 5,000. But it is not over yet for this continuing story of Jesus authority over Creation. After the people had eaten Jesus sent His disciples across the Sea of Galilee in a boat. He stayed on the shore to send the people away and then he went up onto a mountain to pray.

It was a long trip across the sea in the boat. The wind and the sea were contrary, blowing against disciples efforts to reach to the other side. When it was almost morning the disciples thought they saw a ghost walking on the sea. But it was Jesus walking on the water towards them. We have grown to love Peter, he is so bold. Peter often illustrates how we are, but sometimes he does things no one else would do. Peter called out to Jesus *"if it is you command me to come to you on the water"* (Matt 14:28). Now Peter had just seen Jesus heal many people and he had just seen Jesus feed the 5,000 so there is an apparent belief that Jesus has authority over all things and Peter believed Jesus could enable Peter to walk on the water. Jesus said to Peter *"come"* and so Peter stepped out of the boat onto the water and started to walk to Jesus ON THE WATER. Unfortunately Peter looked to the side, taking his eyes off Jesus looking at the waves and winds. And, so Peter began to sink into the water. Peter called out to Jesus *"Lord save me"* and Jesus immediately stretched out His hand and pulled Peter out of the water. There Peter heard Jesus say *"O you of little faith, why did you doubt?"* When Peter and Jesus stepped into the boat the winds and waves ceased (Matt 14:22-33). And they were immediately at the land where they were going (John 6:21).

In this story Jesus demonstrates His authority in that;

- He fed the multitudes with a blessing
- He has power over the winds and waves of creation by His spoken word
- He is not constrained by the physical world
- He can even instantly transport a boat and 12 disciples to the place he wants

This sequence demonstrated His identity to His disciples through His authority over creation. They had just seen Him feed 5,000. Now they saw Him still the winds and the waves by His spoken command causing the disciples to ask the question *"Who can this be, that even the winds and the sea obey Him?"* (Matt 8:27). They were beginning to understand Jesus was more than a prophet. As the Creator He spoke and fed 5000. As the Creator He spoke and the wind and sea were stilled. As the Creator He spoke and enabled Peter to walk on water. As the Creator He transported the boat to its destination in an instant.

2.2.2 Power to heal the sick

Another proof of Jesus as the Creator and King is illustrated through the miracles of healing he did to so many sick and ill during the 3 years of His teachings. He healed through prayer, He healed by touch, He healed by instruction, and He healed by the spoken word. The Gospels are full of examples of Jesus healing the sick and we are told by witnesses that Jesus healed many more times than are even recorded in the Gospels. The Apostle John states there were so many things that *"Jesus did that the world itself could not contain the books that would be written"* (John 21:25). There were days, such as the day Jesus fed 5,000, when he healed and taught all day long. The individual healings of that day are not recorded. So we will only review a few of the stories of healing that are recorded in the Gospels.

<u>Jesus healed the blind</u>

Jesus demonstrated His authority and identity through healing many blind people. In one case Jesus was passing by the city of Jericho. A blind man was sitting by the side of the road begging. As the crowd passed by there was a lot of noise and commotion as there were a large number of people. The blind man could not see what was happening and why there was such a large crowd. So because of all the noise he asked those passing by what was happening; why were all these people passing by, what was all the commotion about. When they told him that Jesus of Nazareth was passing by he cried out *"Jesus, Son of David, have mercy on me"* (Luke 18:35-43). He was certainly not ignorant about what Jesus had been doing, healing the sick and the blind as by this time He was quite famous.

Jesus stopped walking and commanded the people to bring the blind man to him. The blind man called Jesus Lord and said *"Lord, that I may receive my sight"*. Jesus just simply spoke to him *"receive your sight, your faith has made you well" (Luke 18:42)*. Immediately the man received his sight. All the people in the crowd gave praise to God when they saw Jesus heal this blind man.

Jesus simply spoke and the blind man was able to see, demonstrating His authority over creation.

<u>Jesus healed physical ailments</u>

Again there was a large crowd gathered around Jesus as he walked. There was a woman who had had a flow of blood for twelve years. This was not only painful for her but in their culture made her unclean. If a woman had a bloody discharge from her body she was to be considered unclean and all she touched was considered unclean. Furthermore whoever touched the things she touched was considered unclean (Lev 15:25-27). So this woman was in a most pitiful position.

When she heard about Jesus she came up from behind Him in the crowd and touched Jesus garment. For she had said *"If only I may touch His clothes, I shall be made well"* (Mark 5:25-34). Immediately the "fountain" of blood was dried up, and she felt the healing in her body.

Just a touch of His clothes she thought. That is how much faith she had. Just the touch healed.

Jesus was aware that she touched Him and felt the power going out of Him that healed her. He turned and said *"Who touched My clothes"*? Now Jesus disciples did not understand and remarked; the crowd is all around you and you ask who touched My clothes?

As Jesus turned around to see who had touched His clothing the woman trembled with fear. She came and fell down before Jesus and told Him the whole truth, the reason and what she had done.

Jesus said *"Daughter, your faith has made you well. Go in peace, and be healed of your affliction"*.

Just the touch of even the garment Jesus wore healed the woman because she had faith in Jesus authority over health.

2.2.3   Authority to forgive sin

Jesus demonstrated something only God can do; forgive sins. No priest, no statue of stone, no ancestor, no saint who has gone before us, no words, no sacrifice or act of men can forgive the sins of men. But Jesus has authority to forgive sins.

<u>Paralytic forgiven AND healed</u>

Up in the northern part of Judea near the upper end of Galilee Jesus had entered into a house. Because of His fame so many people gathered that there was no longer room in the house for any more to enter. Even the door was blocked so no one could see Jesus. It was to this crowd that four friends came carrying a man who was paralyzed. No one could wiggle through the crowd by themselves. Surely four men carrying a cot with a paralytic would not be able to pass. But these four men were determined to put their friend in front of Jesus so they went up on the rooftop of the house and broke through the ceiling. Then they let the cot down into the room where Jesus was.

Here Jesus made a statement that shocked the people and angered the Pharisees. Jesus did not immediately address the sickness of the man but the sins of the man. The Scripture (Mark 2:1-12) tells us that Jesus focused the thoughts of the people on sin and the forgiveness of sin. These four friends had made a great effort to put their paralyzed friend in front of Jesus. Why, because they believed that Jesus had the authority and ability to heal. They believed if Jesus saw their friend He would heal them. Jesus saw their faith, their faith demonstrated by their actions.

Jesus did indeed heal their friend but first he focused on sin. Jesus said *"son, your sins are forgiven you"* (Mark 2:5).

As we can expect, the enemies of the Gospel, the Scribes were listening. Jesus heard their thoughts "who can forgive sins but God alone?" (Mark 2:7). Jesus then questioned the Scribes as to why they were thinking these things. He asked them *"Which is easier, to say to the paralytic, 'Your sins are forgiven you,' or to say, 'Arise, take up your bed and walk'?"*(Mark 2:9). Jesus explained to them the purpose of Him saying your sins are forgiven you was; *"that you may know that the Son of Man has power on earth to forgive sins"*. Then Jesus told the paralytic, to get up, pick up your bed, and go to your own house. (Mark 2:10, 11) The paralytic immediately took up his bed and walked.

Jesus purpose here was that they/we would know that that Jesus, the Son of Man, the Son of God, has authority to forgive sins. He expanded their understanding of His authority beyond just physical healing. A prophet might be able to heal by the power of God. But only God can forgive sins.

Not only did Jesus forgive the sins of the man He heard the thoughts of those sitting there thus demonstrating His authority as God.

<u>Adulteress woman forgiven</u>

Another story in which Jesus demonstrates His authority to forgive sins involves a woman who was brought to Jesus by the Pharisees to test Him (John 8:1-11). They had literally caught her in the very act of committing adultery. This was a serious offense. So serious that the law in Leviticus said that both the adulterer and adulteress should be put to death (Lev 20:10).

An interesting part of this story is that according to the law both the adulterer and adulteress should be put to death. If the woman was caught in the very act then there was a man who was also caught in the very act. Where was the man who was committing adultery with her? According to the law the man should be stoned also.

The Pharisees quoted Moses and the law, that such should be stoned. Testing Jesus they asked what do you say, hoping to trap Him. But Jesus did not answer or speak to them. Instead He stooped down and wrote on the ground with His finger as if he had not heard them. They continued to ask Him so He raised Himself up and spoke; *"He who is without sin among you, let him throw a stone at her first"* (John 8:7). Then Jesus stooped down again and wrote on the ground. As Jesus wrote each of the accusers left, being convicted by their conscience beginning with the oldest. We are not told what Jesus wrote on the ground. Possibly He wrote some laws on the ground the first time. Possibly He wrote on the ground the second time the names and sins of each accuser from the oldest to the youngest.

In any case all the accusers were convicted of their own sin and left. When Jesus stood up He asked the woman who accuses you. She said; no one Lord. Jesus does not specifically say that He forgives her sins here but Jesus tells her; "Neither do I condemn you; go and sin no more" (John 8:11). There cannot be a lack of condemnation without forgiveness. So He did forgive her sins. By the words Jesus spoke we see His purpose was; to save, not condemn *"For God did not send His Son into the world to condemn the world, but that the world through Him might be* saved." (John 3:17)

Jesus demonstrated His authority to forgive sin by the lack of condemnation. But not only that; He demonstrated His authority in the knowledge of the hearts, behaviors, and sins of her accusers.

2.2.4 Power over life and death

Jesus not only healed the sick but He demonstrated His authority by raising the dead, not just once but several times (Luke 7:11-15, John 11:1-43). For us this is significant as we are all destined to die. Anyone who had the power to raise someone from the dead would have to be looked at as God. This sets Jesus apart from common man and at least puts Him in the class of the prophet Elijah. For who else would have the power over life and death other than God, the Creator.

The most famous of these stories of Jesus raising the dead is the story of Jesus raising Lazarus from the dead. Jesus had spent some time with Lazarus and his two sisters Mary and Martha. It was known that Jesus loved them. So when Mary and Martha sent a message to Jesus to tell Him that Lazarus was sick it surprises us that Jesus did not immediately go to heal Lazarus. He loved Lazarus and had shown many times that He could heal the sick. He could surely have gone and healed this man He loved. But He stayed two more days in the place where He was. We find that His delay was purposeful so that Lazarus would die and in that be able to show His authority over death.

When Jesus arrived in Bethany at the house of Mary and Martha, Lazarus had been dead for four days. They had already wrapped Lazarus in funeral clothes and buried him in his tomb. First Martha ran out to meet Jesus. Martha tells Jesus that if He had been there Lazarus would not have died. Martha and Jesus exchange some very important words that have great meaning and value to us.

> *Jesus said to her, "Your brother will rise again. "Martha said to Him, "I know that he will rise again in the resurrection at the last day. "Jesus said to her, "I am the resurrection and the life. He who believes in Me, though he may die, he shall live. And whoever lives and believes in Me shall never die. Do you believe this? "She said to Him, "Yes, Lord, I believe that You are the Christ, the Son of God, who is to come into the world." (John 11:23–27)*

For all mankind these words identify Jesus as the source of life. He has the authority over life and death. Jesus is "the resurrection and the life". Martha believed Jesus could heal the sick. She believed in the resurrection in the last day. She believed that Jesus was the Christ, the Son of God. But she did not know Jesus himself is the resurrection and the life.

The story goes on with Jesus going to the tomb and asking for the stone to be taken away. Martha told Him, by this time there is a stench. Lazarus body will have been decaying and would already stink from death. Jesus looked up to heaven and spoke to the Father giving us a clue of His purpose in raising Lazarus in the words He spoke to the Father when He said *"And I know that You always hear me, but because of the people who are standing by I said this, that they may believe that You sent Me"*. Then with the spoken words "Lazarus come forth" Lazarus emerged from the tomb still wrapped in grave clothes.

Through this miracle Mary and Martha and all who were there saw that Jesus had the power over life and death. They had known He could heal the sick. Now they saw He could raise the dead. This miracle was so demonstrative of His authority that the Jews sought to kill Lazarus and the testimony of his resurrection by Jesus (John 12:9–11).

Jesus demonstrated his authority over death in bringing life to Lazarus. He did so through the spoken word that we might believe the Father sent Him.

2.2.5   Authority over demons and spirits

One of the most powerful testimonies of the authority of Jesus is that all demons and spirits obey Him. They not only knew Him as the Son of God, they said so, and they obeyed Jesus. There are a number of stories told in the Gospels of Jesus authority over demons. These demonstrations of the authority of Jesus over demons is summarized with these words; *"And demons also came out of many, crying out and saying, "You are the Christ, the Son of God!" And He, rebuking them, did not allow them to speak, for they knew that He was the Christ."* (Luke 4:41)

In one of the recorded stories Jesus was in the synagogue and there was a man there possessed by a spirit. This spirit within the man cried out *"What have we to do with You, Jesus of Nazareth? Did You come to destroy us? I know who You are—the Holy One of God!"* (Mark 1:24). Jesus rebuked the unclean spirit and commanded it to come out of the man. The spirit convulsed the man cried out in a loud voice and came out of the man. The people there were all amazed asking; *"with authority He commands even the unclean spirits, and they obey Him"* (Mark 1:27).

This story reveals to us that the unclean spirit knew Jesus. The unclean spirit called Him Jesus of Nazareth. It knew His name and knew Jesus birthplace. The unclean spirit also called Jesus the Holy One of God. .

The spirit obeyed Jesus. It could not refuse the command of Jesus because Jesus was the Son of God, the Holy One of God. The people were amazed that just by His spoken word the unclean spirits obeyed him.

In another recorded story there was a man possessed by a legion of demons (Mark 5:1-17). A legion would be around 2,000 demons. Jesus and His disciples had just crossed the Sea of Galilee after having completed teaching on the other side. He had just demonstrated His authority over Creation, stilling the sea by rebuking the wind and the sea with His spoken word.

As soon as they come out of the boat they were met by this possessed man. He lived among the tombs. Because of the many demons within him he was very strong. No one could bind him. They had often tried to bind him with shackles and chains but he pulled them apart. Night and day he lived in the mountains and among the tombs crying out and cutting himself with stones.

When this man saw Jesus from a far distance he ran to Jesus and worshiped Him. Jesus told the unclean spirit to come out of the man. At first the unclean spirit responded by saying *"what have I to do with You, Jesus, Son of the Most High God? I implore You by God that You do not torment me*" (Mark 5:7). When Jesus asked the demon its name it replied "**My name is Legion; for we are many**" (Mark 5:9). The demons then begged Jesus not to send them out of the country but into a herd of swine. Jesus gave them permission and they entered the swine, about 2000 of them. The swine immediately ran violently down the steep slope into the sea and drowned. The owners of the herd of swine came and found the one who had been possessed sitting, clothed, and in his right mind.

This story reveals the authority Jesus has over the demons and their view of who Jesus is.

1. Great numbers of demons in no way diminish Jesus authority. They went into a herd of swine numbering 2,000. One demon – one swine. That is a lot of demons. A legion of 2,000 demons feared Jesus and obeyed Him without question.
2. This legion of demons ran to Jesus when they saw him – from far off. They ran and bowed down to Him. They knew who had authority, Jesus! They had to bow before the Son of the Most High God even though they did not want to. They begged Jesus not to torment them. They knew Jesus had authority to do to them whatever he wanted. He could have sent them to the bottomless pit to be locked up forever.
3. The demons identified Jesus as the Son of the Most High God
4. The demons did not question or challenge the authority of Jesus. They knew He was beyond challenge of authority.

Jesus has power and authority over all things including demons, spirits, and Satan the father of lies. Whom then should we fear, "*He who is in you is greater than he that is in the world*" (1 John 4:4).

2.3 Testimonies of the King's Identity

In any court of law in the World the testimonies of eyewitness accounts to an event are used to determine truths. Most laws require more than one witness testify.

There are many witnesses who testified that Jesus is the Son of God. We will look at; Jesus disciples, a Roman military commander, John the Baptist, Jesus Himself, and God the Father's testimony as He speaks. But we must begin with the Old Testament prophecies Jesus fulfilled that identify Him as the King.

2.3.1 Prophecies fulfilled by the King

No collection of evidence that Jesus is the Christ is complete without including the topic of prophecies. There are 333 prophecies in the Old Testament that Jesus fulfilled in His life on Earth. Multiple prophets and authors were given these prophecies about the coming Messiah. A very small list of those prophecies is:

- The prophet Daniel prophesied that there would be 173,880 days from the command to restore and rebuild Jerusalem until the Messiah the Prince would enter Jerusalem (Dan 9:25-26). This happened just as prophesied with Jesus riding into Jerusalem 173,880 days after Cyrus the king of the Medes and Persians gave the command for the children of Israel to go and rebuild the walls of Jerusalem.
- The prophet Zechariah, prophesied that the coming King will ride into Jerusalem on a lowly donkey (Zech 9:9). That He did so is told in (Matt 21:1-5).
- The Messiah would be born of a virgin (Isaiah 7:14) as told in (Luke 1:26-32).
- That Jesus would be born in Bethlehem (Micah 5:2) as told in (Luke 2:4-7).
- The details of Jesus death, pierced hands and feet yet bones are unbroken, the casting of lots for His clothing are prophesied in (Psa 22:16-18) as told in (John 19:24).
- Jesus would be buried in the potter's field bought with thirty pieces of silver (Zech 11:13) and confirmed in (Matt 27:6-10).

We cannot avoid Isaiah Ch 53. It describes Jesus sacrifice, crucifixion on the cross, His payment for our sins. *"⁵He was wounded for our transgressions, He was bruised for our iniquities; The chastisement for our peace was upon Him, and by His stripes we are healed". "⁷He was oppressed and He was afflicted, Yet He opened not His mouth; He was led as a lamb to the slaughter". ⁹And they made His grave with the wicked but with the rich at His death, because He had done no violence, nor was any deceit in His mouth". "¹⁰Yet it pleased the LORD to bruise Him; He has put Him to grief. But it pleased the Lord to bruise Him". "¹¹By His knowledge My righteous Servant shall justify many, for He shall bear their iniquities."* As told in; (Jo 19:1-30)

All these prophecies predicting the Messiah were written 1,400 to 400 years before they were fulfilled by Jesus life on earth.

Only God could accomplish this

2.3.2   Jesus disciples

As Jesus was coming into the region of Caesarea Philippi, He asked His disciples *"Who do people say that the Son of Man is?"* So they answered that there is a mixed understanding by the people on who Jesus is. Some say John the Baptist, some Elijah, some Jeremiah, or one of the prophets. Jesus followed up by asking *"But who do you say that I am?"* Peter spoke for the disciples *"You are the Christ, the Son of the living God"*. (Matt 16:13-17).

Peter testified before Jesus crucifixion that Jesus is the Christ. Afterward Peter gave a sermon testifying that Jesus is the Christ (Acts 2:14–38). Peter's testimony that Jesus is the Christ is sealed when Peter gave his life was crucified because of his testimony.

It must be noted here that all of the disciples gave their lives in violent deaths because they believed in Jesus as the Son of God. They were crucified, beheaded, and killed by the sword. Only one, the Apostle John, lived to an old age but he was said to have been boiled in oil, survived, and sent into exile.

2.3.3   The centurion

The commander who was over the Romans carrying out Jesus crucifixion was convicted by what he saw. He would have seen how Jesus responded to his accusers. He would have seen how Jesus responded when they beat Him. He would have seen how Jesus reacted to having the nails driven through His hands and feet. Then when Jesus cried out on the cross and died there was an earthquake, graves were opened, and the dead came out of the graves and walked about the city. The Centurion and those with him were in great fear and the Centurion said *"Truly this was the Son of God!"* (Matt 27:50-54)

It was how Jesus walked through the accusations, abuse, and torture of the cross. Now it was as if Creation itself spoke that this was the Son of God. Not a Jew, the Centurion testified that by what he saw of Jesus that Jesus must be the Son of God.

2.3.4   God the Father testifies

The greatest testimony of all was through God the Father's words when He said this is my Son. He spoke the words saying this is My Son both at Jesus baptism and at the transfiguration on the mountain when Moses and Elijah appear with Jesus. The Father said: *"This is my Beloved Son in whom I am well pleased"* (Matt 3:17) at his baptism. *"This is my Beloved Son in whom I am well pleased, hear Him"* (Matt 17:9) on the mount of transfiguration.

Jesus Baptism

At the time of Jesus walking on the earth John the Baptist was teaching in the wilderness saying *"repent, for the kingdom of heaven is at hand"* (Matt 3:2). When people asked John who he was, Elijah or the Prophet he quoted Isaiah 40:3 saying he was the voice of one crying in the wilderness saying *"make straight the way of the Lord"*. John told them clearly he was neither Elijah, nor the Christ. Of course the Pharisees asked him then why do you baptize seeing you are neither the Christ, nor

Elijah, nor the Prophet? John responds telling them that I baptize with water but one is coming who baptizes with the Holy Spirit.

So on a day John the Baptist was baptizing in the Jordan River north of the Sea of Galilee. Jesus came to John to be baptized but John said; I need to be baptized by You and are You coming to me? Jesus spoke *"Permit it to be so now, for thus it is fitting for us to fulfill all righteousness"* (Matt 3:15).

When Jesus was baptized the heavens were opened to Him, and He saw the Spirit of God descending like a dove and landing on Jesus. Then a voice came from heaven saying "***This is My beloved Son, in whom I am well pleased***" (Matt 3:17), (Mark 1:11, Luke 3:22). What greater testimony is needed to identify Jesus as the Son of God than to have God the Father say so? The heavens were opened up as a testimony. The Holy Spirit descended like a dove to identify Jesus as a testimony. And God the Father spoke calling Jesus His beloved Son as a testimony.

The transfiguration

Not just once but twice God the Father identified Jesus as His Son.

The second time is when Jesus took Peter, James, and John up on a high mountain by themselves. There Jesus was transfigured before them. He was shown to them in His glory. His face shone like the sun and His clothes became white as the light. Then two of the most revered of men from Jewish history, Moses and Elijah appeared with Jesus talking with Him (Matt 17:1-3).

There Jesus was glorified before them, giving them a glimpse of Jesus as God in His glory. This all took place with Elijah representing the prophets of God through history and Moses representing the law given by God

Our bold Peter was captured by the transfiguration and spoke out of his wonder and passion. He said it is good to be on the mountain in this place. Then he also said let us build three tabernacles in this place; one for Jesus, one for Moses, and one for Elijah. There was no reprimand or encouragement for Peter by Jesus. It would look like Peter would worship Moses and Elijah along with Jesus. The answer was given in the demonstration of God's glory and the words from the Father. While Peter was still speaking *"a bright cloud overshadowed them; and suddenly a voice came out of the cloud, saying, "**This is My beloved Son, in whom I am well pleased. Hear Him!**"* (Matt 17:5). Not only was Jesus glorified in the shining light of his face and clothing, and the bright cloud that overshadowed them but He was identified by the Father as His Son. This is reminiscent of God's glory coming down on the tabernacle in the wilderness. God had told Moses that He would meet with the children of Israel in the tabernacle that God would sanctify with His glory (Ex 29:43). This is reminiscent of the glory of the Lord coming down and filling the temple when Solomon completed its dedication (2 Chr 7:1-2). Here it is God's glory showing through His Son.

But the voice of the Father spoke. *"This is My beloved Son, in whom I am well pleased. Hear Him!"* We already discussed the significance of Moses and Elijah being present demonstrating the transition of God's interaction with men from the prophets and the law to Jesus. Here the point we want to bring out is that the Father verbally testifies that Jesus is His beloved Son. With that identification the Father instructed mankind to listen to the words of His Son Jesus.

Peter later testified.

> *For we did not follow cunningly devised fables when we made known to you the power and coming of our Lord Jesus Christ, but <u>were eyewitnesses of His majesty</u>. For He received from God the Father honor and glory when such <u>a voice came to Him from the Excellent Glory</u>: "**This is My beloved Son, in whom I am well pleased**." And we heard this voice which came from heaven when we were with Him on the holy mountain.* (2 Pet 1:16-18)

2.3.5   Jesus Testifies

It is not just the miracles, not just the works of Jesus, or only the voice of God (although that is clearly enough) that testifies that Jesus is the Son of God. Jesus makes His own claim to be the Son of God. His claim coupled with all His works and the testimony of God and the witness of men say we should listen to His words that say He is the Son of God.

John the Baptist who baptized Jesus was there when a voice from Heaven spoke and said *"This is My beloved Son, in whom I am well pleased"* (Mat 3:17). But later when John was thrown in prison he sent two of his disciples to ask Jesus if He was the Coming One, or should they look for another. Jesus did not say specifically that He was the Son of God or the Coming One but by implication through these words *"**Go and tell John the things which you hear and see:** The **blind see** and the **lame walk**; the **lepers are cleansed** and the **deaf hear**; the **dead are raised** up and **the poor have the gospel preached to them**" (Matt 11:4-5)*. Jesus implied that He was the Coming One. The evidence through His authority over all things speaks for Him. Jesus is saying the evidence of His works makes it clear He is the Coming One.

At another time the elders of the people including chief priests and scribes brought Jesus into their council and asked Him "If You are the Christ, tell us" (Luke 22:67). Jesus did not answer that question directly but said they would not believe Him if he told them who He was. So they asked Him "***Are You then the Son of God***" (Luke 22:70). This time there is no mistake who Jesus claimed to be as he answered "***You rightly say that I am***" (Luke 22:70). In His own words Jesus claimed He is the Son of God.

Just before Jesus crucifixion Pilate, the governor, asked Jesus *"Are You the King of the Jews?"* Jesus said to him, *"It is as you say."* (Matt 27:11). Here Jesus says He is the King of the Jews.

Jesus also makes claim to being God through this statement *"Most assuredly, I say to you, before Abraham was, I AM"* (John 8:58). Jesus claims that He is the "I AM", God Himself.

So Jesus testifies that; 1) He is the Coming One as evidenced by His works, 2) He is the Son of God, and 3) He is the King of the Jews, 4) That He is God, the "I AM".

2.3.6   Jesus resurrection

The culmination of the testimony that Jesus is the Son of God and rules with all authority and power came through His death and subsequent resurrection from the dead. This is so important to us because it is through His death that our debt to sin is paid and it is through His resurrection that we have life eternal. There were many that testified to His resurrection. He first appeared to Mary Magdalene. Then he appeared to two of the disciples as they walked into the country. Later He appeared to the eleven disciples as they sat at the table. (Mark 16:9-14).

But His appearances did not end there. He appeared to the disciples at the sea where they were fishing and demonstrated who He is again through a miracle of a great catch of fish (John 21:3–10). Later Paul testifies to the list of people who saw the risen Jesus. *"He was seen by Cephas (Peter), then by the twelve. After that He was seen by over five hundred brethren at once, of whom the greater part remain to the present, but some have fallen asleep. After that He was seen by James, then by all the apostles. Then last of all He was seen by me (Paul) also"* (1 Cor 15:3-8).

2.4   Summary identification of Jesus Christ as the King

So who is Jesus Christ? He is:
- The Creator
- The Son of God
- The Coming One
- He is the King of the kingdom of God
- The "I AM"

The evidence for this was demonstrated through:
- His authority over Creation
- Through healing miracles
- His authority over spirits
- Through fulfilled prophecies

- The testimonies of first hand eyewitnesses accounts
- The voice of the Father Himself
- The claims of Jesus Himself
- The testimony of the Apostles

Jesus the King of the kingdom of God

He has taken a seat at the right hand of the throne of God (Heb 12:2)

Jesus is the King that is rebuilding His Kingdom, He is building the church, as we will see. Jesus told Peter *"I will build my church"* and *"I will give you the keys of the kingdom of heaven"* (Matt 16:18-19).

3   The Kingdom of God (Kingdom of Heaven)

As a reminder of why we are seeking the kingdom of God we go back to the Gospel of John where Jesus tells Nicodemus *"Most assuredly, I say to you, unless one is born again, he cannot see the kingdom of God"* (John 3:3). This statement raises the idea of there being a kingdom of God that we might visit. If we believe that there is a God and that he has a kingdom it raises all manner of questions.

- What is the kingdom of God?
    - Is it a physical kingdom?
    - Is it a spiritual kingdom?
- Where can the kingdom of God be found?
    - Is it a physical kingdom on Earth?
    - Is it a physical kingdom in Heaven?
- When will the kingdom of God be established?
    - Does it exist now?
    - Is it in the future when Jesus rules the Earth for 1000 years?
    - Is it even further in the future after Jesus 1000 year reign?

What are the people like? What is the language? What is the currency? How are they governed, is it a monarchy, a democracy, a tyrannical system? What are the entry requirements?

A good travel agent would have researched the proposed destination and be able to give potential travelers all kinds of information regarding the king, its residents, its fruit, and its lodging. In actuality who would listen to a travel agent unless the travel agent had visited that destination himself. Preferably a citizen of that land. Who then is that travel agent? Where then can we find travel brochures telling us of this land? The place we turn to are the words of the King of the kingdom himself and through the witness of citizens of the kingdom of God, as recorded in the Bible.

Knowledge of the kingdom of God is an important topic, after all preaching the Kingdom of God was central to the teaching of Jesus Christ (the King) and His Apostles (citizens). Jesus, the King of the kingdom of God said *"**I must preach the kingdom of God** to the other cities also, because **for this purpose I have been sent**"* (Luke 4:43). The king came to tell us of His kingdom.

First John the Baptist preached that the kingdom of God was at hand (Matt 3:1-2). Then Jesus preached that the kingdom of God was near (Matt 4:17). Jesus told the Pharisees where the kingdom of God could be found; in you (Luke 17:21). Later in his ministry Jesus said people were pressing into the kingdom of God (Luke 16:16). Then after His resurrection Jesus spent time with the disciples *"speaking of the things pertaining to the kingdom of God"* during the 40 days after His resurrection (Acts 1:3). Throughout His ministry Jesus demonstrated the importance of the kingdom of God to Him.

Knowledge of the kingdom of God is important to the King, He came to preach it, and to impart knowledge of the kingdom to His disciples. If Jesus preached it then we will find information about the kingdom in the Gospels, recorded for us so that we might understand it and teach it to others.

Not only did Jesus say that he came for the purpose of preaching the kingdom of God, He also sent out His disciples to preach the kingdom of God. In one recorded instance Jesus called His twelve disciples together and gave them power and authority over demons and the ability to heal the sick. But he sent them out for the purpose *"to preach the kingdom of God"* (Luke 9:1-2). After that Jesus sent out seventy others, two by two, to preach that the kingdom of God has come near you (Luke 10:9).

It is clear that knowledge of the kingdom of God is important to Jesus

It would stand to reason that if Jesus sent His disciples out to preach the kingdom of God it should also be a primary message shared by today's follower of Christ. Therefore, we must understand the kingdom of God so that we also may preach it. The instruction *"All authority has been given to Me in heaven and on earth. Go therefore and make disciples of all the nations, baptizing them in the name of the Father and of the Son and of the Holy Spirit, teaching them to observe all things that I have commanded you; and lo, I am with you always, even to the end of the age."* (Matt 28:18-20) is for every believer to carry out. So that *"this gospel of the kingdom will be preached in all the world as a witness to all the nations, and then the end will come"* (Matt 24:14)

It is the responsibility of every believer, every citizen, to preach the kingdom of God

So what does this mean to make disciples and baptize them in the name of the Father, the Son, and the Holy Spirit in relation to the preaching the kingdom of God? We find that the objective of the seeking to save that which was lost goes hand in hand with the knowledge of the kingdom of God. For it is seeking the lost that they might enter the kingdom of God.

3.1   What is the Kingdom of God

We all think of a kingdom in terms of a region of land over which a king or government rules. We see physical boundaries that separate the kingdom from other kingdoms and lands. Within the kingdom there are citizens who work the land, trade with each other, and serve the king. The king also provides a service to the people in the form of protection and in infrastructures no individual can build by himself.

There are by example good kingdoms where a benevolent king earns the respect of his people through his love and service to the people. These people honor their king and will obey his commands. The king of Thailand was such a king serving as monarch for 70 years. He was loved and respected by his people, so much so that at 6PM each evening music played the kings anthem and wherever the people were they stopped, stood still and honored their king. Before a movie began the kings anthem was played while all stood up to honor their king. The level to which the people respected this king was demonstrated during a riot. A rebel group had barricaded themselves in Bangkok for a couple of weeks. When the king spoke and said it was enough both sides stopped, cleaned up the streets and went back to their business. He earned this respect through the years by his service to the people and the "king's projects".

The "kings" projects which demonstrated his care for the people of Thailand. He died in 2016 and the country of Thailand mourned for a full year.

There are also by example tyrant kings who rule over their kingdoms by force and oppression. The people of these lands serve their king only out of fear. Usually these are military leaders and dictators who have overthrown governments and ruled for their own purposes of power, control, and to fill their own pockets. The corruption within the ranks and government branches in this country never generate peace as there is always an underlying element of conflict. The lifestyle of these nations always degrade into a poorer state of living for all of the people, including the rulers.

But what about the kingdom of God? Is the Kingdom of God a physical kingdom, or is the Kingdom of God a spiritual kingdom?

Jesus gives us many illustrations of the Kingdom of God through His parables. He starts these parables with the words *"The kingdom of heaven is like"*, or *"to what shall I liken the kingdom of God"*. Jesus wanted us to know what the kingdom of God (heaven) is like. He spent quite a bit of time describing it. So we will look at what the kingdom of God is like by reviewing the parables Jesus told.

> Note: the kingdom of heaven and the kingdom of God are the same thing. Matthew uses the words "kingdom of heaven" but Mark, Luke, and John use the words "kingdom of God" in reference to the same parables. When Jesus sent out the disciples to heal the sick and to preach; Matthew records this as the "kingdom of heaven" (Matt 10:7), Luke records this as the "kingdom of God" (Luke 9:2). Then the passages in Matt 13:11 and Luke 8:10 link the kingdom of heaven to the kingdom of God as being the same subject of His parables.

> *Matthew 13:11 [11] He answered and said to them, "Because <u>it has been given to you to know the mysteries of the kingdom of heaven</u>, but to them it has not been given.*

Luke 8:10 ¹⁰ And He said, "To you <u>it has been given to know the</u> *<u>mysteries of the kingdom of God,</u> but to the rest it is given in* *parables, that 'Seeing they may not see, And hearing they may not* *understand.'*

Clearly the "kingdom of heaven" and the "kingdom of God" are the same.

Jesus uses many parables to illustrate what the Kingdom of God is like. These illustrations help us understand the nature of the kingdom as;

- He teaches about the King, about Himself. What does the King value? What is important to the King? How does the King behave?
- He teaches about the citizens and the laborers. He gives illustrations of citizen's behaviors, both good and bad.
- He teaches about the coming celebration when the Kingdom is complete.
- He teaches how the Kingdom's boundaries are being enlarged. How are the kingdom's borders defined and how are they being expanded.
- He teaches on the requirements necessary to enter the Kingdom.
- He teaches on the responsibilities of its citizens.

<u>The King's values</u>

The first place we should look for an understanding of what constitutes the kingdom of God is by studying what interests the King of the kingdom of God. Is the King interested in lands? Is the King interested in minerals? Is the King interested in manufacturing? Is the King interested in wealth?

Jesus stated His interest is in retrieving the lost souls of men. That which the King engaged in throughout the ages in the greatest love story ever told. That which was lost when sin entered into the world through Adam and Eve. Recovering His people from the distrust and disobedience planted in their hearts by Satan in the Garden of Eden.

The message of the kingdom of God is just the opposite of distrust in God. Death and separation came through distrust and reliance on self. Salvation comes through belief and trust in Him. That is why Jesus says *"I must preach the kingdom of God to the other cities also, because for this purpose I have been sent"* (Luke 4:42–43).

It is because the King, *"the Son of Man has come to seek and to save that which was lost"* (Luke 19:10). What is it that was lost? The souls of mankind was lost. From the time of the first sin in the Garden of Eden man was lost.

If the King's interest lies in the finding that which was lost, the souls of men. Then the King would desire to fill His kingdom with that which He treasures. Therefore the kingdom of God must be made up of or populated by the souls of men.

That the King's interest lies in the souls of men is further solidified by the parables Jesus told in describing what the kingdom of heaven (God) is like. For example; the parable of the sower and soils and the parable of the dragnet clearly point to acquiring souls of men as the purpose of the Kingdom of God. We will examine these parables in greater detail in a later chapter. Here we want to use these parables to point out that the kingdom of God is focused on the souls of men. This is important to us when we look to interpret the parables describing the kingdom of God.

<u>The parable of the sower and soils</u>

Three of the Gospels (Matt 13:1-23, Mark 4:1-20, Luke 8:4-15) record this parable of the sower and soils. This parable illustrates a sower going out and spreading seeds everywhere. Some seeds sprout and produce fruit. Other seeds have problems for a number of reasons and do not produce fruit.

This is one of the parables that Jesus clearly interprets and explains. Because Jesus explains this parable is about the hearts and souls of men it is clear that the kingdom of God is about the souls of men. The seed is the Word of God. The soils are the hearts of men. Some accept the

Word with joy while others do not, and still others are drawn in by the desires of the world.

This parable makes it clear that the kingdom of God involves the activity of planting the Word of God in the hearts of men.

<u>The parable of the Dragnet</u>

In this parable Jesus illustrates the kingdom of heaven by describing a fishing net in the form of a dragnet. (Matt 13:47-50) This net is pulled through the sea collecting all the good fish along with the bad fish. When the net is pulled in the fishermen separate out the good fish and burn the bad. This parable describes the kingdom of God as a drawing in of the souls of men. As Jesus explains; souls of men who at the end of time will be sorted out by angels, separating the wicked from the righteousness.

<u>The kingdom of God is not of this physical world</u>

Finally Jesus tells us *"My kingdom is not of this world"* (John 18:36) in answer to Pilate's question if he is the King of the Jews. His kingdom is not made up of the physical regions of this world.

So we can conclude that the kingdom of God is made up of the souls of men and the activity of the kingdom of God is the drawing of the lost souls for the King.

3.2   Where is the Kingdom

Where then is the kingdom of God where the souls of men reside. Is it in some physical place on Earth where these souls will reside sometime in the future? Is it in some spiritual place, like heaven, where the King is collecting the souls of men?

Jesus tells us where the kingdom of God is when He answers the Pharisees question *"when the kingdom of God would come"* (Luke 17:20). Jesus tells them that the kingdom of God is not something you can see come, in other words it is not a physical kingdom with boundaries or lands. You can't stand on a hill and see the kingdom of God as you can see the kingdom of Thailand from Myanmar or Laos. Neither is the kingdom of God some land or place in the present or future. Rather Jesus tells them *"the kingdom of God is within you"* (Luke 17:21).

This fits with what the King is interested in, the souls of men, their hearts. We are told *"you are the temple of God", that the Spirit of God dwells in you"* (1 Cor 3:16). We begin to understand more clearly that the kingdom of God, where the King resides and rules is in the hearts and souls of men.

Just like any kingdom that has been established there is a price that was paid for the land which is part of the kingdom. In the kingdom of God the hearts and souls of men were purchased by its King, for *"you were bought at a price; therefore glorify God in your body and in your spirit, which are God's"* (1 Cor 6:20).

- The King, Jesus, has bought us with a price – we belong to Him
- When we believe in Jesus Christ as our Savior the Holy Spirit comes to live within us
- The King then rules the kingdom of God that resides within our hearts

The kingdom of God is located where the Holy Spirit dwells, in the heart of a believer.

So the "WHAT/WHERE" is the kingdom of God can be defined this way:

The Present Kingdom of God; Or, less frequently, "kingdom of heaven" (such as in Matthew), is the kingly rule of God in the hearts of people. It refers to the acceptance of Jesus as Savior and recognition of the authority of the King who rules there. It is not a geographical area but resides in our hearts, our hearts that were purchased by Jesus Christ with a great price, His life. It began with Jesus Christ as its first fruit in His resurrection. At the end of time Jesus will deliver this kingdom of God to the Father.

3.3 When is the Kingdom

In trying to determine when the kingdom of God is established we look through the whole Bible to see what is said about the kingdom of God. We find the phrases "kingdom of God" and "kingdom of heaven" are not found in the Old Testament. But in the New Testament they appear 207 times.

Since the kingdom of God and the kingdom of heaven are not mentioned in the Old Testament but are mentioned 207 times in the New Testament it would indicate that the kingdom of God comes after Christ. Indicating a "church age" kingdom.

The first words about the kingdom of God come from John the Baptist. He came preaching in the wilderness saying *"repent, for the kingdom of heaven is at hand"* (Matt 3:1-2). This was closely followed by Jesus *"Jesus began to preach and say, repent, for the kingdom of heaven is at hand"* (Matt 4:17).

Both John the Baptist and Jesus said that the kingdom of God (Heaven) is near in time, when they say it is at hand. From these words we confirm that the kingdom of God was not during the Old Testament times and had not yet come. But the time of the kingdom of God was about to come.

Then Jesus clearly draws the line between *the* Old Testament times and the nearness of the coming kingdom of God when He states that *"the law and the prophets were until John. Since that time the kingdom of God has been preached, and everyone is pressing into it"* (Luke 16:16). He delineates between the time of the teaching of the law and prophets and the time of the teaching of the kingdom of God. The kingdom of God was first preached by John the Baptist and Jesus and so people were pressing (desiring) to enter the kingdom of God but the door was not yet open. We will see that the kingdom did not start until Jesus was resurrected from the dead.

This is explained in 1 Cor 15:20-24; *"But <u>now Christ is risen</u> from the dead, and <u>has become the firstfruits</u> of those who have fallen asleep. For since by man came death, by Man also came the resurrection of the dead. For as in Adam all die, even so in Christ all shall be made alive. But <u>each one in his own order</u>: <u>Christ the firstfruits</u>, <u>afterward those who are Christ's at His coming</u>. Then comes <u>the end, when He delivers the kingdom to God the Father</u>, when He puts an end to all rule and all authority and power"*.

Jesus Christ through His death and resurrection is the first fruit of the resurrection. The first of the kingdom of God, the King Himself. Then afterwards those who belong to Christ, the believers are added to the kingdom one by one in order of belief. First the disciples and then those who believe in Christ because of their testimony throughout time. Today it is us. This is what has been happening since Jesus rose from the dead. Then at the end of time Jesus will deliver the kingdom of God to the Father. The kingdom of God where the Spirit dwells and the King rules - in the heart of the believer.

As a further explanation as to when the kingdom of God comes there are additional verses that show it began with Jesus resurrection.

> Jesus explains that the kingdom of God has not yet come at the Passover dinner before His crucifixion. He said *"With fervent desire I have desired to eat this Passover with you before I suffer; for I say to you, I will no longer eat of it until it is fulfilled in the kingdom of God."* (Luke 22:15-16). From this we would look to the time when Jesus again breaks and eats bread to confirm that the kingdom of God has come.

> It is after Jesus resurrection from the dead that He appears to His disciples and eats in the presence of the disciples. *"Now it came to pass, as He sat at the table with them, that He took bread, blessed and broke it, and gave it to them"* (Luke 24:30). Later in this same passage (Luke 24:40-43) Jesus eats physical food.

In between these two events the kingdom of God had come. Jesus died on the cross purchasing the hearts of those who would believe in Him with His blood. Then Jesus rose from the dead being the first fruit of the kingdom of God, opening the door for all who would enter through Him as He had said *"I am the door of the sheep"* (John 10:7-9). The door through which all must enter into the kingdom of God.

When John the Baptist and Jesus were preaching before Jesus Christ was resurrected, the kingdom was near. Since His resurrection the kingdom has been growing in the heart of every new believer. Every believer's heart being a possession of the King, purchased by His blood, and part of the kingdom.

This sequence is illustrated in *Figure 1*.

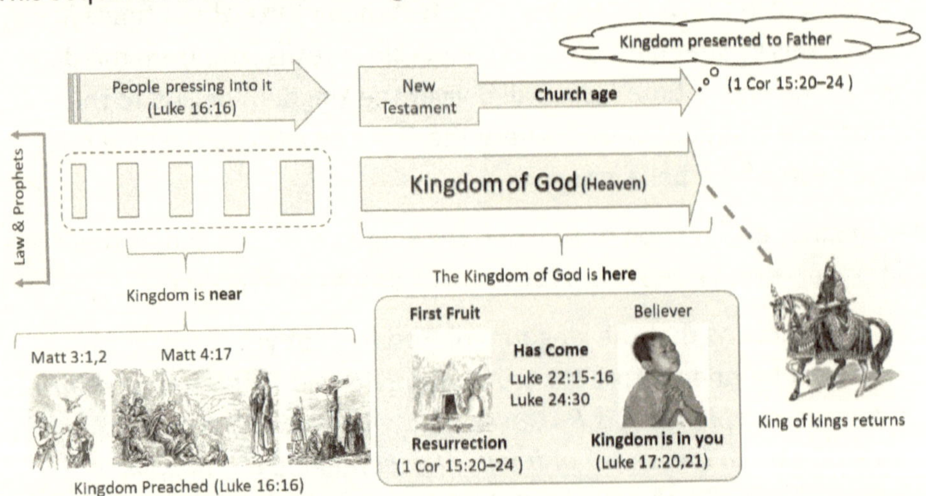

Figure 1, Time of the Kingdom of God

1) John the Baptist began preaching that the kingdom of God is near (Matt 3:1-2).
2) Jesus began preaching that the kingdom of God was near (Matt 4:17).
3) Jesus preached that the law and prophets were until the time of John the Baptist but since then the kingdom of God has been preached and everyone is pressing into it (Luke 16:16).

4) Jesus explains that the kingdom of God resides in the believer (Luke 17:20-21).
5) Jesus tells the disciples He will no longer eat of the vine until it is fulfilled in the kingdom of God (Luke 22:15-16).
6) Jesus died and was resurrected becoming the first fruit of the resurrection and the kingdom of God (1 Cor 15:21-24).
7) Jesus broke bread with the disciples after His resurrection signifying the kingdom of God has begun (Luke 24:30).
8) The door, Jesus, was opened so that all who will can enter through Him (John 10:7-9)
9) Before Jesus went up to heaven Jesus spent 40 days with the apostles speaking of the things pertaining to the kingdom of God (Acts 1:3).
10) Jesus continues to build His church, the kingdom of God as each one is added in order (1 Cor 15:21-24, Matt 16:18).
11) At the end of time Jesus will present the kingdom of God, the church, to the Father (1 Cor 15:21-24).

When then is the kingdom of God?
- It was near when John the Baptist began preaching the Gospel of our Savior
- It began when Jesus rose from the dead
- It grows in the hearts of each believer
- The kingdom is being built today as it was from the time of Jesus resurrection
- The kingdom age is the church age defined as those who believe in Jesus Christ
- It will continue to build till Jesus returns – when He delivers it to the Father
- This is when Jesus puts an end to all other rule, authority, and power

4   Entrance into the Kingdom of God

We have been telling the story of a loving King and the magnitude of His love we want everyone to grasp. He has been working since the beginning to prepare for His kingdom. He did not abandon His people but continually reached out to His people to bring them back to Himself throughout history. Then He paid the price of redemption for the rebellion of His people by shedding His own blood and dying on a cross. He rose from the dead having power over death and so gave life to those who would believe in Him and so launched the building of the kingdom of God. All these things the King did while He walked on the earth demonstrating His loving and compassionate nature. As John the Apostle said; *Behold what manner of love the Father has bestowed on us, that we should be called children of God!* (1 John 3:1)!

We have already discussed the; what, when, where of the kingdom of God. Now we will look at what it takes to become a citizen of the kingdom.

The King has sent out an invitation and given the qualifications necessary for citizenship. This invitation is being spread around the world by its current citizens as they export from the kingdom the fruit of Spirit *"love, joy, peace, longsuffering, kindness, goodness, faithfulness, gentleness and self-control"* (Gal 5:22-23).

Now is the time to apply for citizenship. Be warned, there is a limit in time to when we can apply. We must do so in our lifetime. And as we do not know the time of the end of our lifetime, if we do not apply today we may never gain entry.

We have some questions about entering a kingdom;
1) Can you see a kingdom without entering the kingdom?
2) Can you enter a kingdom without permission from the king or government?
3) Can anyone take up residence or become a citizen of a kingdom without meeting the qualifications of that kingdom?

How can someone enter the Kingdom of God?
1) Has the King of the Kingdom of God sent out an invitation?
2) What are the qualifications that the King has set?
3) How can I become a citizen of the Kingdom of God?

4.1   Awareness of the Kingdom

It is pretty obvious that you cannot see a kingdom without entering. Viewing it from a distance, reading a brochure, or hearing someone tell of it would be your first awareness that the kingdom even exists. Through brochures or tales of its citizens you can't feel, smell, savor the wonders of its fresh fruit, sleep there, or live there. Everything rests on your imagination painted there by words from its citizens; pictures of its land and people, and maybe a taste of fruit that has been exported. You can't see it close up. You can't walk down the street. You might visit with a citizen who is traveling through the world and hear what he tells of his kingdom. But you can't really see a kingdom or know and understand a kingdom without entering into it.

This makes it a bit difficult to explain the kingdom to a non-citizen because all he will hear is what is told him. All he will taste is the fruit of the Spirit of the kingdom lived out by those citizens with whom he comes into contact with. But the taste of the fruit of the kingdom of God is not like any other.

He might see how its citizens treat each other. He might hear someone sing an anthem to their King. He might even overhear a phone call (prayer), from a citizen to the king. But unless He is a citizen He is not likely to understand; what is being shared, spoken, or felt. He won't even understand what is being said as he doesn't speak the language. He really can't see the kingdom until he enters it and walks around in it. He would not even know where this kingdom is. Even worse he might not even be aware of this wonderful kingdom's existence. The only knowledge of this kingdom must come from its citizens, travelers through his city, who are exporters of the fruit of the kingdom of God.

Remember what Jesus said? *"The kingdom of God does not come with observation; nor will they say, 'See here!' or 'See there!' For indeed, the kingdom of God is within you."* (Luke 17:20-21). He told us that the kingdom of God is in the person who believes in Jesus as His Savior, as the Son of God. The kingdom is in each believer's heart! It is a spiritual kingdom. It is a place the King purchased with His own shed blood. You can't see this kingdom with your eyes, but it is here and it is growing and expanding. The citizen of the kingdom of God is then an exporter of the fruit of the kingdom of God, the fruit of the Spirit.

4.2   Permission to enter the Kingdom

We asked a 2nd question; can you enter a kingdom without permission from the king or government? Well no! Governments don't generally allow foreigners to enter without permission. You need a passport that identifies you. But beyond this passport you must also bring an invitation letter, and must obtain a visa from the kingdom you wish to enter. You must receive a seal that is stamped on the passport at the time of entry. A seal of authority from the government. Anyone who tries to come in by another way has attempted to enter illegally and will be denied. Some countries today fail to follow their laws and have broken immigration systems. But not the kingdom of God. Denial is assured for the kingdom of God to those who do not carry the seal of the Spirit.

Those who would enter must have an Invitation from the King

It is pretty unheard of that a country will send out invitations for people to come and settle there.   Years ago there were some countries that offered land for settlers to come and take up residence, but not today. Today, only if there is a benefit to the country will they send out invitations. They may advertise for tourism and will try to make the tourist comfortable. They will sell the reason to come as a benefit to the tourist, but the underlying purpose is to bring in money to the country sending out the invitation. They have no motivation to send out invitations to help the people who might come to become citizens.

But what about the Kingdom of God? Is there an invitation to for us to come and become citizens? And, if there is an invitation is it only for certain kinds of people, those with certain kinds of skills, those with impeccable character? Is there a limit to how many can come?

Actually yes, the King has sent out an invitation for citizenship. His Spirit and the citizens of His kingdom say "come" (Rev 22:17). Those who hear this message and become citizens will also say "come" to others as they taste of the King, His nature, and His love.

The king has planned a wedding feast. He has sent out invitations. But many who received the invitations have rejected the invitation with excuses of being busy with personal matters. So the King has commanded His servants to <u>invite all those they can find</u> (Matt 22:8-9). The invitation is to the poor, the rich, to the criminal, everyone. This includes us, our neighbor, our boss, and even our enemy. He has sent the invitation to those who had never even heard of the King.

This coming feast is for those who have entered the kingdom of God. The marriage feast of the Lamb of God, the King Jesus, to his bride, the Body of Christ. Those who have entered the kingdom of God will be the bride at the marriage supper of the Lamb of God, to the King of the kingdom of God (Rev 19:9). They will become fully "one" (Jo 17:20-21) with the King at this wedding. The Church, the kingdom of God, the body of Christ is the bride.

The invitation is being sent to all people and those who come to the wedding feast will be the ones who have accepted the invitation to enter the kingdom of God.

The kingdom of God has one door, only one, by which someone can enter.

Every country has designated places where people can enter legally. You can't just enter at any place along the border. At those official ports of entry those who would enter must present their invitation papers or visas. Immigration officers at the entry points check for passports, visas, and invitation letters. If all is in order the immigration official places a stamp of entry on his passport.

The kingdom of God also has an entry point. Just one. The kingdom of God also has a door keeper. The door, the doorkeeper, and the King Jesus Christ are the same. The King Himself is the door by which we can enter (John 10:7-9). He is also the one who provides the seal, the guarantee for entry, the Holy Spirit (Eph 1:13).

There will be many who will come to the King after their final hour expecting to enter the Kingdom. They will even call Him Lord. They will tell of all their works and their deeds. Some will say they prophesied in the name of the King. Some will even say they cast out demons in the name of the King. But the King will tell many *"I never knew you; depart from Me"* (Matt 7:21-23). They do not carry the seal of the Holy Spirit.

We might describe this in our everyday terms. Lord; I went to church every Sunday, I tithed 10%, I taught Sunday school for 20 years. Lord I gave to the poor, I prayed for my family. But it is not our works that qualify us for entry. It is <u>who the King knows</u> that will be granted entry. To others His words will be *"I never knew you"*. It is a painful embarrassment to be denied entry into a worldly kingdom but it is death to be denied entry into the kingdom of God.

Jesus tells us who it is that will enter the Kingdom, *"he who does the will of My Father in heaven"* (Matt 7:21). There we see one of the keys to entering the kingdom – to know and do the will of the Father of the King. But this passage in Matt 7 also says it is those whom the King knows that will enter the kingdom of heaven. All those things we might have done in serving as a work that we think is a proof of being citizens of the kingdom may all be unrecognized by the King.

So we ask the question; then how do I know He knows me? It is also written *"if anyone loves God, this one is known by Him"* (1 Cor 8:3). Therein lies the next question; do we love the King. The Word says if we love the King, He knows us. This circle brings us back to the 1st and greatest commandment Jesus gave. We must love the Lord our God with all our heart, with all our soul, and with all our mind (Matt 22:37). The outcome is that if we love the King we will do His commands, which is the Fathers will (John 14:15). This completes the circle of His love generating our love for Him and then because we love Him we do the Fathers will. Not our will but the Father's will.

> *Those who desire to enter must put all their trust in the King, accept His purchase price*

> *They must love the King*

> *If they love the King they will do the will of the King's Father in heaven*

Those who would enter the Kingdom must desire to let the King rule

Those who desire to enter must be willing to come under the rule of the King. That means a life in which <u>HE IS MY King</u>. King over all their thoughts, their deeds, and their desires. A place where only one King rules. It is not a democracy where the people vote or make laws. It is not a place where two kings rule and share authority. No, only the Creator King has all authority. So that means those who would enter must trust the King completely and accept His will in all things. They must become like little children who believe their parents love them and put all their trust in them. Anyone who wants to enter the kingdom of God must, just like a little child, become fully dependent on the King (Matt 18:3-4). The condition of their heart is humility before the King.

All who would enter the Kingdom of God must have been sealed as citizens of the Kingdom.

When a person enters a country they receive a stamp (an official government seal) on their passport. Then any officer or agent seeing the seal accepts that the person has legitimately been qualified by the government for entry into the country. Just like the passport needs to carry the seal of the government into which a person has been granted entry, those who enter the kingdom of God also must also have a seal of the Kingdom of God in order to enter.

When a person is presented the gospel of the Kingdom of God, when he hears it and understands it, when he believes in the King and accepts His purchase price, and when he trusts in the King then he receives the seal of the Holy Spirit from the King. This seal is the guarantee of entry and inheritance into the kingdom of God (Eph 1:13-14). This is the Kingdom of God passport stamp, or seal that guarantees the believer has been granted entry into the kingdom. But this seal has much more value as it also declares and guarantees that he is now a citizen of the kingdom. Not just a visitor or tourist.

Those who desire to enter must have their names written in the King's book, the Lamb's Book of Life.

The King keeps a list of names of everyone who has become one of His citizens. When the King restores His final physical kingdom only those who have their names written in His Book of Life can enter (Rev 21:27). Only those who are clean and without sin can enter. We know our present state. We are not clean of ourselves in our hearts. But, it is because we have believed in the Son of God, Jesus, who is the King that we are qualified. That we have trusted in Him, because He has paid for all our sins. We have been washed and cleaned into perfection by the King Himself. The believer is spotless before the Father because of the washing through His Son, the King.

It is the King who puts a soul's name into the Book of Life. This occurs when that person believes in Him, and puts his trust in Him.

Differences between the kingdom of God and the kingdoms of man

1. The invitation to the kingdom of God is to the benefit of those who chose to come.
   - When a kingdom of man or a country invited people to come they desire the visitor's money so they can build up their kingdom for themselves
2. The invitation to the kingdom of God is because of love
   - The invitation into an earthly kingdom is for self and greed
3. Those who enter the kingdom are heirs to the kingdom

- Earthly countries do not make foreigners heirs much less allow them to own property in their nation

4. Those who come to the wedding feast are the bride of the King
    - Only dignitaries and leaders from other countries will even see and meet the president of an earthly country. No one would offer a hand in marriage except to make a treaty of peace for their own advantage or mutual advantage.

4.3   Qualifications for citizenship

All countries have qualifications for citizenship. They are measures of how the applicant will behave in their country, how he will conduct business, how he will treat his neighbor. So the person's life and history is examined. Only if he is does not have a criminal record and has values in agreement with that country will he be offered citizenship. And that only after he has been taught the laws of the country, has been examined for his knowledge of them, and pledges allegiance to the country.

The kingdom of God also has qualifications but they are not measured in the quality of the applicant but upon the quality of the King. In futility man has through the ages continued to try to gain entry into the kingdom of God by living a good life but he cannot meet the standards of the holiness of the kingdom of God. Neither can man pay for his sins through any sacrifice or merit he performs to gain entry. He is unable to gain entry into the kingdom on his own. It is only through what the King has done. Only by having believed in the King and by placing his faith in the King, Jesus Christ, is he made worthy of entry into the kingdom (Gal 2:16). Worthy because the King paid the price of death on the cross. Worthy because it is the King's robe of righteousness (Isa 61:9) bestowed upon the believer that is the qualification for the believer to enter the kingdom of God. Worthy because the believer has the seal of the Spirit within him given to him by the King.

Jesus begins the description of the qualification for entry into the kingdom of God beginning with *"unless one is "born again" he cannot see the kingdom of God* (John 3:3).

Jesus completes his description of the qualification for entry into the kingdom of God by explaining that it is the work of God through sending His Son to pay for the sin of rebellion and that by simple acceptance of believing in Jesus as the Son of God a man is saved (John 3:16).

In between Jesus explains that being *"born again"* is a spiritual birth. Man was created with a body, a soul, and a spirit in the image of God. Man was created to live in a dual reality; physical interactions with creation, and spiritual interactions with his Creator. That was the condition in the Garden before man was led into rebellion against the King, his Creator.

Nicodemus, as do we, only understands the physical birth into which we are born to interact with this world. But Jesus explains that a second birth is necessary to restore the intended relationship with God. This is a spiritual birth of the Spirit. We have all been born into this world by being born of the flesh. The second birth is an act of the Spirit. Jesus explains *"That which is born of the flesh is flesh, and that which is born of the Spirit is spirit"* (John 3:6). The spiritual birth is required in order to interact with the other reality.

Being born of the flesh produces children of the flesh. The *"children of the flesh, these are not the children of God"*. Being born of the Spirit of God produces children of God. *"But the children of the promise are counted as the seed"* (Rom 9:7-8). Children of the promise of belief and faith in the Son, the King. Only those who are born of faith are counted as children of God according to the faith. Not as descendants through the flesh but as children of the promise through faith in Jesus Christ.

This new creation is from above, from God. It has been birthed through hearing of the word of God *"having been born again, not of corruptible seed but incorruptible, through the word of God which lives and abides forever"* (1 Peter 1:23). It is of faith, through the hearing of the word.

This *"faith comes by hearing, and hearing by the word of God"* (Romans 10:17). This faith acknowledges that Jesus is the Lord and believes that God the Father raised him from the dead. It is not superficial but comes from the heart. *"if you confess with your mouth the Lord Jesus and <u>believe in your heart</u> that God has raised Him from the dead, you will be saved. For with the heart one believes unto righteousness, and with the mouth confession is made unto salvation* (Rom 10:9–10).

Then the seal of qualification, the Holy Spirit, comes to indwell the believer as the guarantee of this new birth. *In Him you also trusted, after you heard the word of truth, the gospel of your salvation; in whom also, having believed, you were sealed with <u>the Holy Spirit of promise, who is the guarantee of our inheritance</u> until the redemption of the purchased possession, to the praise of His glory* (Eph 1:13–14). We do nothing to be born of the Spirit other than believe, it is a gift from God to us when we believe in Him. The Holy Spirit is His seal within our hearts identifying that we belong to Him, like a seal on our passport.

This spiritual birth is not reincarnation for as it is written *"it is appointed for man to die once"* (Heb 9:27). Furthermore *"Flesh and blood cannot inherit the kingdom of God; nor does corruption inherit incorruption"* (1 Cor 15:50).

This spiritual birth is not by baptism. *"Whoever believes that Jesus is the Christ is born of God"* (1 Jo 5:1). This scripture does not say one is born again by baptism. It does not say one is born again of the flesh. It says those who believe are born of God. John the Baptist came preaching repentance and baptism with water. But John the Baptist distinguished between the water baptism unto repentance and the baptism of the Holy Spirit through Jesus Christ (Matt 3:11).

Baptism is a public expression by a believer that he desires to be identified with Christ. It is an outward declaration by the believer that He has chosen to follow the King. The choice for baptism by the believer is much like the choice made by a bondservant described in the OT (Ex 21:5–6). If a slave was set free because his debt was paid he might choose to remain with his master. Most likely because he loves and respects his kind master. They would have a ceremony in front of the judges declaring that this servant chooses to remain in service to his master voluntarily. His ear would be pierced as a mark so that all who see him know that he belongs to his master by his own choice, of his own free will. He is now identified as a bondservant a willing servant, by choice to that master. Baptism is a similar declaration to others that the believer has chosen to be identified with the King who has paid his debt and set him free. Now because of love he chooses to become a bondservant of the King.

<u>Conclusion</u>

The qualifier for entry into the kingdom of God is being "born again".

The trigger for being born again comes from hearing the Word and believing that Jesus Christ is the Son of God. That Jesus died on the cross to pay the debt of sin. That Jesus rose again from the dead.

This new believer receives the seal of the Holy Spirit as a guarantee of entry into the kingdom of God as a child of God, a citizen of the kingdom.

Being born means that there is a new life. But the "born again" spoken of by Jesus in John 3:3-8 is a greater birth than we normally think. A new believer *"is in Christ, he is a new creation; old things have passed away; behold, all things have become new"*. It is *"of God, who has reconciled us to Himself through Jesus Christ"* (2 Cor 5:17–18). He is a new creation not of man but of God. This new creation cannot be observed with physical eyes much like the kingdom of God cannot be seen. Jesus illustrates this by using the wind to describe being born of the Spirit. *"The wind blows where it wishes, and you hear the sound of it, but cannot tell where it comes from and where it goes. So is everyone who is born of the Spirit"* (John 3:8).

4.4   Application for citizenship

How do we apply for citizenship?

The Father has already done all the work for us to become part of His kingdom. It is the *"Father, who has qualified us to share in the inheritance … for He rescued us from the domain of darkness, and transferred us to the kingdom of His beloved Son, in whom we have redemption, the forgiveness of sins"* (Col 1:12–14). The Father sent His Son out of His mercy and love. His Son Jesus came and has paid the full price of entry with His death. It is the Spirit that convicts and seals the believer for His kingdom. Only one thing remains, we must believe in Gods Son, the King. We must accept His gift that He offers to us. It is so simple and yet so hard.

It is simple in that we must only believe. Just the opposite of rebellion, we surrender to the King. We let go of trying to rule. We let go of trying to make sufficient sacrifices that we might think would earn enough merit to enter the kingdom. We simply accept the King's offer and the price He paid.

It is hard in that we must let go of ourselves. We must agree that we cannot be a king in the King's kingdom. There can only be one king and that King is Jesus Christ, the King who is from the beginning. So we must deny ourselves and humble ourselves before the King (Luke 9:23). That seed of rebellion is so hard to get rid of. It is hard in that we must truly believe "in our heart" that God has raised Jesus from the dead and confess so with our mouth (Rom 10:9-13).

If we but put the little bit of trust or faith we have in Him he is faithful to reward those who diligently seek Him (Heb 11:6) by growing our faith in Him.

5   The nature of the King, His values

We learned a bit about the King, Jesus, by his work throughout history as He appeared to the prophets. We learned more about the King's nature when we looked at His works when He walked the earth where he; made the lame walk, made the blind see, and where the winds and waves, and the demons obeyed Him. These testify to who He is.

He demonstrated what He values throughout history and when He walked the earth by His works and by His own words. His behavior throughout the greatest love story ever told has testified to His delight in righteousness, justice, and longsuffering.

When the King gave Moses the tablets of the law written in stone he showed Himself to Moses and declared; I am the Lord the Lord God. I am merciful and gracious. I am longsuffering. I abound in goodness and truth. I am merciful to thousands, forgiving their iniquity and their sin. But I also judge the guilty (Ex 34:5-7).

Then 1000 yrs later to the prophet Jeremiah He speaks of His nature again. *"I am the Lord, exercising lovingkindness, judgment, and righteousness in the earth. For in these I delight" (Jer 9:24).* It is not just that He does these things He delights in them!

Now let's look at the values of the King from His own words. He described what the kingdom of God is like when He walked the Earth. These stories, parables, speak of something that was lost. They speak of the heart of the One to whom this was lost. They speak of how much He treasures that which was lost. So much that He will risk all He has to bring back that which was lost.

These stories reveal the heart of the King. That great love story written throughout time in which we now are the actors.

5.1   He paid all to purchase a field for the treasure in it

The first parable is very short. All He says is that the kingdom of heaven is like a treasure hidden in a field. When a man finds this treasure He goes and sells all that he has and buys that field. (Matt 13:44).

Someone had taken a treasure and buried it in a field. That treasure was useless while it was buried. No one could enjoy it or use it for any purpose.

This man who finds the treasure buried in the field does not steal it or take it by force but rather buys the field in which the treasure is buried. He sells everything He has to purchase the field for the treasure buried in that field. He does this with joy and happiness in recovering that treasure.

We know that the kingdom of God resides in the souls of men. So this parable speaks of the treasure of the souls of men being buried in the ground, laying in the dark, where they have become useless. This parable speaks of their value as a treasure to the King of kings, Jesus. They were buried there by the enemy, the thief, the destroyer of the kingdom who at the beginning stole them from the King. But the King sold all He had to buy that field for the souls in it. He so loved the souls in the field of the world He gave His life as the purchase price to buy that field. He did not come as a conquering King, taking the kingdom by force. Rather He purchased it with a great price, giving His own life, giving up His exulted position and His presence with His Father (Phil 2:5–8). He paid with everything He had, even being separated from the Father when on the cross He cried out *"My God, My God why have you forsaken Me"* (Matt 27:46, Mark 15:34). It was there He purchased that field with His own blood (Acts 20:28). Out of that field is found the church, the treasure of the kingdom of God.

In the field of souls in the world is the precious treasure of the church, bought with all He had including His own life. Not as a conquering king but as a King purchasing the land.

5.2   He paid all to purchase one precious pearl

This parable is also very short. Again it tells of having found something of great value and the one who having found it sells all he has to buy that item.

In this story the kingdom of heaven is like a merchant looking for beautiful pearls. When he finds one that has a great price he sells all he has and buys that pearl (Matt 13:45).

Here the King likens Himself to a merchant seeking beautiful jewels. He finds one that is very valuable. It must be a pearl extremely precious to what the King values, what he sees, what He treasures in His heart. Like in the story of the treasure found in the field He sells all He has and buys that one pearl of great price.

Again we see that the King so valued this pearl that He sold all He had, His life, His position on the throne of God to purchase that one soul. This was the great price necessary to purchase that one pearl. This expresses the heart of the King in the great love story. He treasures each and every individual soul so much that He gave all He had just for one. Yet He did it for many but the beautiful pearl of your soul alone was enough for Him to sell all He had.

The King values the treasure of each individual soul that is added to His kingdom more than He valued his position on the throne of God in glory and His own life.

5.3   He values every soul like just one lost coin

This parable describes a woman who had ten silver coins. She lost just one of those coins. So she lit a lamp to see where it might have fallen. The house was dark as in the time of Jesus houses had few if any windows. Not finding it with the light she got out her broom and carefully swept the whole house to search for the one lost coin with the lamp in her hand. In her careful search she found this one lost coin. So joyful over finding the ONE lost coin she called her friends and neighbors together to celebrate over finding that ONE lost coin out of the ten she had (Luke 15:8-10).

What the King is telling us in this parable is how much ONE soul is valued in the kingdom of God. He is telling us how diligent He is in searching to recover that one lost soul. He will search the whole house. He will sweep the whole house. The bigger house that is the world.

This parable illustrates the value of that one lost soul being found as demonstrated in a celebration at the throne of Heaven. Just ONE soul is so valued that *"there is joy in the presence of the angels of God over one sinner who repents." (Luke 15:10).* Joy celebrated together with the angels before God over just that ONE sinner repenting and being restored to the kingdom.

Another glimpse of the greatest love story ever told through the joy in the recovery of one lost soul.

5.4   As a shepherd he seeks that one remaining lost sheep

At one time Jesus sat down to dinner with tax collectors. Tax collectors were known to cheat and take bribes. So the religious leaders judged Jesus for associating with those who do such evil. They thought Him to be unrighteous because He sat, He ate with, and talked with these sinners.

So Jesus told them a parable of the lost sheep. He asked them; which of you if you had 100 sheep and lost one would not leave the 99 and go out looking until he finds that ONE lost sheep. When he finds that ONE sheep he picks it up and carries that ONE sheep home on his shoulders rejoicing along the way. When he arrives home he calls all his friends and neighbors to say "rejoice with me for I have found my sheep which was lost" (Luke 15:1-7, Matt 18:10-14).

This parable again illustrates the value of every single lost soul in illustration through the work of a shepherd. Every sheep is valuable to the shepherd. When He finds the lost sheep He does not walk behind it to drive it home. He picks it up and carries it back home into the kingdom of God. The sheep has lost its way. It is weak from being separated from the food and water. It is in danger of being taken by wolves. He carries the sheep home on His shoulders giving it comfort, safety, and strength that it does not have.

In this parable Jesus clearly identifies the lost sheep as a sinner and states *"I say to you that likewise there will be more joy in heaven over one sinner who repents than over ninety-nine just persons who need no repentance"* (Luke 15:7). Like in the parable of the coin that was found, the ONE lost soul that is found brings more joy to heaven than anyone who does not need repentance. This He tells those who think they are more righteous than others, to remind them what the King values, the souls of each and every man.

This parable not only illustrates the value of one lost soul to the King. It also illustrates the kindness and care of the King, the shepherd of souls, through the manner in which he brings the sheep home.

5.5   The love of a father with two rebellious sons

The stories of the lost coin, the lost sheep, and the story of a lost son were all told to the religious leaders who were judging Jesus for eating with tax collectors and sinners. This parable of the father with two rebellious sons found in (Luke 15:11-32) is the longest of those that illustrate what the King values. It has been called the parable of the lost son or the prodigal son. But it is actually a story that illustrates the nature of the King, the nature of a lost son out in the world, and the nature of a son lost at home. It describes two differing behaviors between the sons and how the King deals with each one individually.

In this parable the younger son asked the father to give him his inheritance while the father was still alive. The younger son took his money and went to a far country. There he wasted his money living wildly. When a severe famine came to that land to the younger son had nothing to eat, no place to live, no place to earn a living. To survive the younger son took a job feeding swine. You have to understand according to the Jewish laws swine were unclean. You could not eat of the swine so feeding them was also unclean. But being hungry and not being given anything to eat he ate of the food given to the swine.

Then he remembered his father. None of his father's servants would go hungry. His father would provide even the servants with bread to eat and shelter for their heads. His father would have bread to spare and yet here he was starving. So he reasoned he would go back to his father and beg for forgiveness for having sinned against him. He would say I am no longer worthy to be called your son. Make me one of your hired servants.

So he went to his father's land. But when he was still a far way off his father saw him and had compassion on him. His father ran to meet him. He wrapped his arms around him, hugged him and kissed him.

The son confessed he had sinned against his father and said I am no longer worthy to be called your son. But the father sent his servants to bring out the best robe and put it on his son. The father told his servants to kill the fatted calf and set up a great feast. Let us be joyful and celebrate he said, for this my son was dead, was lost, but is alive and is found. So they began to celebrate his lost son's return.

Now the older son who had stayed home was working in the fields. He had been loyal to his father and had worked for him all this time serving his father and doing the work in the fields. When he came near to the house he heard the music and dancing from the celebration. So he asked one of the servants what the celebration was for. When the servant told him that your brother has returned so your father has called for a celebration he became angry. He was so angry he would not go into the house. So his father came out and pleaded with him to come and celebrate with him for the return of his lost brother.

The older son told the father of his dedication and hard work. All these years he had been serving the father and yet the father had not put on a celebration for him, but now he killed the fatted calf to celebrate his wayward brother's return. A celebration for the younger brother who asked for his inheritance while the father yet lived. A celebration for the younger brother who took that inheritance and spent it with prostitutes. And now you kill the fatted calf in celebration for him!

The father tells the older son. You are always with me and all I have is yours. The fields the house the money all belong to the older brother at his father's death. It was right to celebrate your brother's return; who was dead and lost but now is alive and found.

There are three parts to this story; 1) the character of the lost son, 2) the character of son who remained, and 3) the character of the father. Each ones behavior tells us something of their hearts. They tell us something about our hearts and the heart of the King.

1) <u>The character of the lost son</u>: He had knowledge of his father's kindness, goodness and love. He had knowledge of his father's commands. He had lived under his father's provision of food and shelter. But his desire was for the world. So he rebelled against the father. He sinned in asking for the inheritance, not accepting what and when the father would give it. He sinned in causing his father the cost of selling his lands to split up the inheritance while He was still living. He sinned in leaving his father, choosing to serve his desires instead of the father.

   But he repented. When he had been stripped of all those desires he had pursued he came to his senses. He went back to his father. He came with a broken and contrite heart to ask nothing more than to be his father's servant.

   We have all been like this, we all once were lost souls. We pursued the desires of our heart from the rebellion put there by the destroyer. We pursued those desires until we were reminded of our father's goodness and love. When we believed in Jesus Christ we came home, just like the son believed in his father.

2) <u>The character of the son who remained</u>: We can be like this son if we are not careful and do not remember from where we came, or it may be that we are in His household yet do not truly know Him. This son labored in the work of the father many years but found himself unable to rejoice when his brother returned and his father celebrated his return. He said he kept his father's commandments all his life but it would seem he forgot his father's love and forgot the 2nd commandment to love his neighbor and brother as himself. If he kept

his father's commandments he would have rejoiced in his brother's return also. He claims to have worked for his father all these years but it might be that all along he instead worked himself, for his future inheritance. It actually sounds like He does not know his father or his father's character of love.

We can all be like this when we begin to think of ourselves more highly than we ought. When we forget that we all were once like the wandering lost son. We can have a tendency to look down on those who have tossed away their belief and chased after the world when they come home.

But we can actually be "lost at home". "Lost at home" pretending that our labors are for the Father when in reality they are for ourselves. Seeking accolades for our good deeds. Seeking respect and positions of authority within the body of Christ. Even to the point of thinking our labors provide credit for our own salvation. Doing so without a love relationship with the King. "Lost at home" not even being known by the Father as Jesus would describe us in (Matt 7:21-13). We might say; I taught Sunday school for 30 years, I tithed 10% all my life, and maybe I went on missions trips each year. Yet we might hear those words "I never knew you, depart from Me".

3) The character of the father is shown: The father let his son choose his path in life. He did not command them like slaves. It was their choice what to do with the inheritance that was made available to them. When his son wanted his inheritance so he could go out in the world the father let him. He took that inheritance and spent it on himself. Yet the Father waited all those years for his son to return. When the son returned to his father to be just a servant the father accepted him back as his own son.

The father saw the lost son coming from afar off. He had been patiently waiting and watching for his sons return. Eagerly yearning for his son. When his son came he ran out to meet him and threw his arms around him showing his affection, forgiveness, joy, and acceptance into the family. He did not wait until the son reached the house, he ran out to meet him. When he had the fatted calf killed and called for a celebration he demonstrated his joy was real for his sons return. He put together a celebration of his sons return with his whole household, like all the angels in heaven celebrating over the return of one lost soul.

However, the older son refused to accept the younger son's return and would not come to the house to celebrate. He was angry for the lack of celebration for himself. He was angry that those long years of service, that those long years of following his father's commands did not warrant a celebration. He looked down upon his brother who had squandered his inheritance on wild living and prostitutes. He told his father so when the father came out to plead with him.

His father reasoned with his angry son that; you are always with me, all that I have is yours, it is right that we should celebrate the return of your wayward brother. It would appear though the older brother who was always with his father he did not really know him. He did not understand his love and compassion. His longsuffering.

The father was forgiving and longsuffering to both brothers. To the one who returned after realizing the true nature of his father and to the one who lived with him but did not know his nature.

This is a picture of our own Father and our King.

He freely gives us the choice to follow Him or rebel and reject Him. It is completely up to us to choose. Our father yearns for our repentance, whether we are out in the world or whether we are lost at home, and waits eagerly and patiently for each lost soul to return to Him. He runs out to those who repent and pulls them lovingly back into His arms. Our father is also patient with those who forget their own need for forgiveness and judge their brothers in self-righteousness. He patiently reasons with them that they might also come into fellowship with Him.

5.6　Summary of the character of the King

The nature of the King and how much He values every single soul is expressed through these parables. The King is not idle in his promise to build the kingdom. He has been and is working to build His kingdom day and night. He is patient towards us, waiting for each soul to return to Him of their own choice and repent of their rebellion. He is actively seeking every single soul and is *"not willing that any should perish"* (2 Pet 3:9). He is so joyful when just one soul returns to Him that He calls the angels together to celebrate with Him.

The question to us is; do we realize how much our soul is valued by the King? He sold all He had to purchase our hearts for the kingdom of God? He gave up His position as God the Creator of the universe and came in the form of a man to pay the debt that man could not pay. That He might live in our hearts to fellowship with us and to talk with us, to be one with us. This nature of His love for us should cause us to *"love Him because He first has loved us"* (1 John 4:19).

Are we the wondering lost son out in the world? Are we the other son "lost at home"?

6   The Labor of the King and the response of mankind

It is the King who is working to build His kingdom (Luke 4:43, Matt 16:18). He is the One who has come to *"seek and save that which was lost"* (Luke 19:10). He has been working since the destroyer came into creation at the Garden of Eden and deceived His people causing them to rebel against Him. Throughout history the King has been speaking, showing, telling, and pleading for His people to return. Finally, as Jesus the King, He came physically to show mankind His love, His nature, and His plan to build the kingdom of God. He calls, He does not force mankind to come into the Kingdom.

The condition, the state of the hearts, of those He is seeking is varied. Some are hard, some hear and forget, some begin to follow but then the desires of this world pull them back. The destroyer, even though he has lost the war is still fighting battles to keep individual souls from entering the kingdom of God.

There are only two kingdoms, the kingdom of God and the kingdom of the destroyer. You may think you are the king of your heart but when you serve yourself you are serving the destroyer and showing allegiance to him and his kingdom.

Jesus also gave us parables that illustrate the condition of the hearts and response of men.

6.1   The Word of God sown in all types of soils/souls

This parable is found in three of the Gospels. It is one of the parables that Jesus explains, leaving no doubt that the kingdom of God is about the souls of mankind.

There was a sower who went out to sow. As he sowed some seed fell by the wayside; and the birds came and ate them. Some fell on stony places where they did not have much earth; they immediately sprang up, but when the sun came up they were scorched because they had no root. So they withered away. Some fell among thorns; and the thorns sprang up and choked them. But others fell on good ground yielding a crop; some a great crop, others a little less, but all yielded a crop. (Matt 13:1-9, Mark 4:1-9, Luke 8:4-8)

The disciples asked Jesus about the parable as they did not understand. Jesus first challenged them, *"Do you not understand this parable? How then will you understand all the parables"* (Mark 4:13)? Then Jesus explained the parable.

He explained that the sower sows the Word of God. The soils are the people's hearts where the Word is sown. **The seed is the Word of God**.

When someone hears the Word of the Kingdom and does not understand it the wicked one comes and snatches away that which was sown in his heart. This is the seed that fell by the wayside and was eaten by the birds. But the ones on the rock are those who, when they hear, receive the Word with joy. But because they have no root they believe for a little while, then when trials and temptation come they fall away from the truth of the Kingdom. The seed that fell among the thorns are those who hear but then are overcome with the cares of this world, the deceitfulness of riches, the desires for pleasures of life. They bring no fruit to maturity. But there was seed that fell on good ground. This seed was heard by those with a good and noble heart who understand and accept it. They bear much fruit with patience. (Matt 13:18-23, Mark 4:13-20, Luke 8:10-15)

This story gives a description of the call to become citizens of His kingdom. It paints a picture for us how people receive the Word of the Kingdom. Some understand, accept, and bear fruit. Others accept it but are caught up with the cares of their daily life and their efforts to satisfy their desires and so do not bear fruit. Some hear the Word but never grow, never sink their roots deeper as they don't seek to know the King and so they stumble and fall. Others only hear the Word like a wind passing by, do not understand it, and so do not give a thought to what it means.

It is not for us to try and determine what kind of soil an individual's heart is and thus choose to only sow in fertile soils. Only the Spirit of God knows the condition of the soil of each person's heart. We must sow the seed of the Word of God everywhere, to everyone.

Soils can also change over time. Where I live in New Mexico we can't grow vegetables in winter because it freezes. Any moisture in my garden soil freezes the soil making it very hard. So when spring time comes the soil is so hard you can't push a shovel into the ground. However if you dump a bit of water on the soil and wait to let it soak in, the shovel can penetrate. A hard stony heart can also be like this. Nothing can penetrate it. But the Word is like the water in the garden. A small bit of the Word left to soak on that hard stony heart may soften that heart over time softening it up to receive a bit more of the Word. Once a bit of soft soil becomes available the soil can absorb larger quantities of water softening it so that you can begin to till the soil. If you keep turning the soil over and over it becomes soft and pliable. With a bit of moisture being added continually it begins to be receive the water more and more readily. In the same way keeping a heart continually tilled with the message of the Gospel will keep it soft and pliable for the Spirit to work. But water evaporates quickly from stony soil and any seeds put on its surface are quickly eaten by the birds. Religiously applying the water is necessary to soften the stony soil.

Shallow soils on top of stony ground are in danger of falling away. In the early spring the sun is warm, the rains have watered the soil so seeds may sprout with the appearance of health and anticipation of fruit. But when the summer heat comes because there no depth the moisture evaporates quickly and the plants wither away and die. Similarly shallow teachings that depend reaching the lost through; relevance, emotion, passion, healings, speaking in tongues, and wealth will not stand when the trials become severe. They have not been provided a Gospel that generates a depth in the soil. This soil has no depth in the Word.

Soils which are not tended are soon overcome by weeds. Those good sounding projects, buildings, programs, and seminars can be those weeds that distract and consume the abilities of the soils to produce. Everyday life involving work, career, children, and possessions can be those weeds that distract the soils from producing. The enemy wastes no time in seeding weeds that consume the water, and the sun to starve the plant from its nourishment. Growth is stagnated. Even though those souls were good soils that could have produced much fruit they have become unfruitful and unattractive as the thorns grow among them. What is needed is a pastor, and elder, a teacher to come along with the correcting hoe watering it with the Word of God to remove those thorns that choke out the souls from producing good fruit.

There are some good soils, deeply founded on the pure Word of God. The purity of the Word provides a resistance to the sprouting thorns choking them out by continually being washed by the water of the Word. In these the fruit of the Spirit is so strong it chokes out the thorns the enemy sows.

After this parable was told the disciples asked Jesus why He spoke in parables to the people. He told them that it has been given to you to understand the mysteries of the Kingdom of God. Later these disciples recorded the truths about the King and the Kingdom of God for us to understand. So, the mysteries of the kingdom of God have been passed on to us to understand.

6.2   Bad seed sown among the good seed

Jesus uses another parable of sowing seeds to explain the kingdom of God (heaven). The kingdom of heaven is like a man who sowed good seeds in his field. But at night his enemy came and sowed weeds among the good seeds. And when the good seeds sprouted so did the weeds. The servants wondered where the weeds had come from, did not the owner sow good seeds. However the owner was not surprised. The owner knew it was his enemy. His servants immediately wanted to go out and de-weed the fields. But the owner tells them they should wait as they might pull out the good seeds with the weeds. He tells them instead to wait till the harvest, then you can easily separate the weeds from the wheat and burn the weeds at threshing time (Matt 13:24-30).

The disciples did not understand this story either, so they asked Him to explain it. So Jesus explained the story to the disciples (Matt 13:36-43).

Jesus explained that the sower of the good seed is the Son of Man Himself, the King of the kingdom of God. The land in which the King is sowing is the world. The world where the rebellious people live along with those who have chosen to give their allegiance to the King. The good seeds are those who believe in the King, that He is the Son of God. They are called the sons of the kingdom of God. The weeds are sons of the wicked one, the deceiver who was the liar from the beginning, Satan. The sons of the wicked one do not believe in the Son of God, but follow the lies of the destroyer, the devil. Those who reject the Son of Man then are the sons of the devil. The harvest is at the end of the age. The angels are the reapers of the harvest, gathering up the sons of the devil for burning in the fire. At the end of time it is the angels who separate the sons of the kingdom from the sons of the devil bringing the sons of the kingdom to live in the mansions the King has prepared for them.

Anyone who has a farm understands this problem. You go out and sow a wheat field. But when it sprouts so also do the weeds. The farmer also knows that while the weeds and wheat are green it is hard to tell them apart. If you were to try to pull out the weeds during their growing time you are likely to pull out the young wheat also. But if you look at a ripened golden brown wheat field the green weeds stand out from among the golden wheat. Then when the wheat is cut along with the weeds the threshing process easily separates the wheat seeds from the weeds.

This parable is again about the souls of men and the harvest. Believers mixed with unbelievers in the world, even within the "churches". The King, the Lord of the harvest and the angels at the end of time separate the believers from the unbelievers. It is the King who sows the fields with the Word of God building the kingdom of God.

Here we see the King at work building His kingdom through His work in the fields of the world. He is continually spreading good seed which grows into maturity. He uses the mature seeds through whom He again sows the seed of the Word to others who might hear. It is at the end of the age when the angels separate the good from the bad and throw the bad, the rebellious people into the fire. At maturity it is easy to distinguish the good from the bad, the sheep from the goats.

We are either sons of the kingdom of God or sons of the devil!

6.3   Summary of the labor of the King/Response of mankind

It is the Word of God that is the seed sown into the souls of men. It is in the hearts of the believer, the good soil, where the word of God matures to produce much fruit. It is also the believer who received the seed of the word of God that matures and produces more seed. At the end of time, when the fields are ripe, the King will give His angels charge to separate the good from the bad, the wheat from the tares.

7   Expansion of the Kingdom

You may not be able to see a kingdom with your eyes but it is possible that you may be aware that the kingdom exists somewhere. If you are not a citizen of the kingdom of God you will not know anything about what it is like except through; what the citizens of the kingdom tell you, a brochure of the kingdom, or the fruit that is being exported by them from the kingdom.

You can learn a lot about a kingdom by the kind of products it exports. You may go to a local farmers market and see the fruits and vegetables grown in an area you have not visited. The oranges may be the best, sweetest tasting oranges in the world. The avocados are the best, freshest, and largest in the world. So not having walked the farms, hills, and villages of that kingdom you may know nothing about that land except that it produces and exports wonderful fruits. Maybe someone in the market will speak the name of this kingdom from where the fruits came. Maybe someone in the market will tell about the people who live in that kingdom and grow and produce these wonderful fruits. Maybe someone in the market will hand out a brochure that tells of the king and the kingdom. But even though you eat the fruit, hear what is told about the kingdom, read the brochure, you still can't get a full picture of that place unless you go there.

This is an illustration of the limited knowledge a non-citizen will have of the kingdom of God. They may be exposed to the fruit of the kingdom of God though the export from a citizen of the kingdom. A very rare and outstandingly tasty fruit when it is fresh without contamination. No other place produces this kind of fruit. The fruit is grown on branches that the King Himself prunes and nurtures. The fruit of this kingdom is; *"love, joy, peace, longsuffering, kindness, goodness, faithfulness, gentleness, self-control"* (Gal 5:22-23). The branches that carry the fruit are the citizens of the kingdom of God. Other kingdoms of this world make cheap copies of the fruit but they are of poor quality and do not last. The fruit of the kingdom of God is the rarest and best. It is the only place where it is produced.

We, in whom the Spirit of the Living God dwells, are the citizens who bring the fruit of the kingdom of God so that others may taste of it. It is only through us, the King's ambassadors, that the fruit is tasted by those not in the kingdom. We, the citizens, as ambassadors of the King bring the brochures as scriptures from the Word of God describing; the King, His call in the greatest love story ever told, and the invitation to become fellow citizens.

As we, who are citizens of the kingdom of God, live among those who do not know the King we are like the parables of the mustard seed and the leaven (yeast) that the King uses to draw believers into His kingdom. So it is very important that we bring only good fruit to touch those around us to leaven that part of the bread as we explain the brochures as scripture passages of the Word to those who might enter. How else will they know of this wonderful King and His kingdom?

7.1   Kingdom is like a mustard seed

Jesus compares the kingdom of God to a mustard seed which when planted grows into one of the largest trees. It is a very tiny seed, about 1 – 2 mm in diameter. In SE Asia the largest tree, the banyan also begins from a very small seed. One of the largest has been determined to cover 14,500 square meters.

Jesus uses this parable to describe the kingdom of God which as a small seed grows and becomes very large (Matt 13:31-32, Mark 4:30-34, Luke 13:18-19).

We have explained that the kingdom of God began with Jesus. Then His eleven disciples plus Paul were added making it 12 Apostles. After that the Lord added to the church daily those who were being saved (Acts 2:46–47). Through time this "tree" of the kingdom of God has grown to around two Billion Christians around the world – a very big tree.

Even the birds of the air come to rest in this tree. The sons of the world, non-citizens, non-believers, come to take shelter in this large tree. They are not of the tree but benefit from its shade and its fruit. They benefit from its lovingkindness, community, and safety without becoming part of it.

7.2 Kingdom is like yeast

Jesus continued His explanation of the growing kingdom using an example of bread (Matt 13:33, Luke 13:20-21). Yeast is added to wheat flower when a cook makes bread. It is the yeast that causes the bread to rise. In comparison to the quantity of flower, it takes but a little bit of yeast. But given a bit of time and some warmth, the flour yeast mix expands as all of the dough is leavened. The yeast grows, multiplies, spreads, and penetrates throughout the dough mix. It is the yeast; that softens the dough, causes it to rise; breaks down starch molecules into simple sugar, strengthening the proteins, and adds to its flavor.

In the same way the testimony of one or two members of the kingdom of God will penetrate those surrounding them, like the yeast in the dough. As time passes, the leaven, the Word is spread by these who have also become believers. So the kingdom of God grows by the believers living in and touching others who live in the world. The testimony of the believers; the fruit of the Spirit, the love of God in them, the Gospel which resides in them, the greatest love story ever told, is the yeast to the unleavened parts of the loaf causing the kingdom of God to grow.

In another passage Jesus also gave the disciples a warning about leaven, bad yeast in the bread (Matt 16:5-12). We are to be watchful regarding religious leaders and teachers. Bad doctrines that come into the loaf and contaminate the bread. This bad doctrine can grow in a church body, like mold in the bread, and destroy it like a virus causes sickness in the physical body.

7.3   Kingdom is like a dragnet

Jesus told the disciples that if they would follow Him He would make them fishers of men (Matt 4:18-19). Later He tells a parable of the dragnet which goes along with the idea of fishing for men.

In this parable Jesus illustrates the kingdom of heaven using a dragnet (Matt 13:47-50). A drag net is a large net that captures anything in the water as it is drug through the water. The net does not select the good from the bad but it gathers all that is in the sea. Most of the dragnets are large enough that they must be pulled through the water between two ships. So in this parable the dragnet picks up bad fish along with the good fish. When the net is full the fishermen take it to the shore and pick through the catch, keeping the good and throwing away the bad.

Jesus likens this picking through the catch to what it will be like at the end of the age. The dragnet of the Gospel of the kingdom has been pulled through the sea of man. It has collected both good and bad. Some who have truly believed in the King. Some who only pretend to be part of the church. At the end the angels will be the harvesters that separate the just from the wicked. The just will go to be with the King for eternity. The wicked will be cast into a fire.

There is a great similarity between this parable and the parable of the tares that grow among the good seeds. In the seed parable, the tares and wheat are not separated until the wheat matures. In the parable of the dragnet the good fish are not separated from the bad fish until the end of time.

This is what we see in the world around us. It is found in those who claim to be part of the church. The wicked are allowed to live with the just. The dragnet of the Gospel of the kingdom draws all of them but only the good respond with ears to hear and to understand. In the end the harvesters, the servants of the Lord will come and separate the wicked from the just. Those in whom the kingdom resides, in whom the will of the King is done will be kept. All others will be thrown into the fire.

7.4   Summary of the expansion of the Kingdom

It is the fruit of the Spirit indwelling the citizens of the Kingdom which is exported into the world giving them a taste of the Kingdom, the taste of which draws those who want to enter. It is love between the citizens. Love from the King of the Kingdom. It is the story of the Kingdom of God and the greatest love story ever told.

It is the yeast of the knowledge of the King, the indwelling of the Spirit that leavens the unbeliever into joining the kingdom of God. This leaven spreads throughout the world. The leaven from the one seed, Jesus Christ, that grows into the large tree of the Kingdom of God.

This Gospel of the Kingdom of God is the dragnet that is drawn through the souls of men to gather those who will choose to become citizens of the Kingdom.

8   The nature of the Citizens, the vineyard and its laborers

All the kingdoms of the world have legitimate citizens. They are citizens by birth or have come through legal immigration. If an immigrant desires to become a citizen they must; first have been invited, second met the qualifications, and third have given allegiance to that kingdom and its king. There are those who want the benefits of that kingdom without allegiance to the King so instead of applying for citizenship they attempt to enter that kingdom illegally. These people may have the appearance of a citizen but because they came by deceit they do not honor the king nor do his will. In the kingdom of God these "attempted entry illegals" will be separated out at the end of the age.

The following group of parables illustrates the nature of the actual and would be citizens; some who wholly honor the king and do his bidding, others who partially give themselves into the king's service, and still others who are not true citizens of the kingdom.

All these parables describe a kingdom, a landowner, and those who would/should be working the fields of that kingdom. Usage of the words "the kingdom of heaven (God) is like" indicates the stories are about the real citizens of the kingdom, the illegal pretenders, and the king of the kingdom of God.

8.1   Citizen laborers of the Kingdom

The parable in (Matt 20:1-16) describes a landowner who owns a vineyard. His vineyard is in need of work. It does not say whether the need is for planting or harvesting, just that the landowner desired to have laborers work his vineyard. The story only tells us about one day in which; the hiring, the labor, and the distribution of wages took place. There is no indication of a yesterday or a tomorrow. It is but one day as it describes the one lifetime of each of the workers called to work the King's vineyard.

The landowner rose early in the morning to hire laborers for his vineyard. He found willing laborers at this early hour, daybreak, and agreed to pay them one denarius for a day's work. Having agreed on the wage the landowner sent the laborers into his vineyard. Later the landowner went out again at the 3rd hour (9AM) and saw other people standing idle in the marketplace. He told them; you also to out to work in my vineyard, and whatever is right I will pay you. He does not agree for wage, nor do the workers ask how much he will pay. They just go to work the vineyard.

The landowner went out again about the 6th hour (noon) and the 9th hour (3 PM) and did the same thing. Hiring more to go work his vineyard and telling them he would give them what is right. Again there was no discussion about the wage, the workers just went out to the vineyard and began to work.

One more time the landowner went out, this time at the 11th hour (5 PM) or about 1 hour before sundown, the end of the day. He found some standing idle and he asked them why they had been standing idle there all day? They answered; no one has hired us. This answer seems to indicate that they were waiting to be asked to work, that they did not go and look for work themselves even though they must have seen there was a need for laborers. Again the landowner sent these laborers out to his vineyard and told them *"whatever is right you will receive"* (Matt 20:7). These laborers also went out to the vineyard without an agreed to wage.

Then when the day was done, when evening came the landowner had his steward call the laborers to give them their wages. The landowner chose to pay the ones who he had hired last first and to pay the ones he had hired first last. He gave each laborer 1 denarius. It did not matter if they labored 1 hour, 3 hours, 6 hours, or had labored all day, all were paid 1 denarius. The ones who had been hired early in the morning were watching the wages being given until their time came. They saw that the laborers who had come later and worked fewer hours received 1 denarius. So they supposed that they would receive more than the 1 denarius they had agreed to since they had labored all day. But when the landowner gave them the same wage, 1 denarius, they complained.

Their complaint was that the last men the landowner hired received 1 denarius but worked only one hour. You paid them equal to us but we labored all day long and through the heat of the day.

The landowner responded. Did you not agree for 1 denarius for a day's labor? If I wish to give this last man the same wage as you is it not lawful for me to do so? My wages are mine to give as I please.

As we read this story and examine it to understand the kingdom of God we see the likeness of the landowner reflecting the King. It is the King who owns the vineyard. If it is the King's vineyard and this story was given to explain the kingdom of God, then the vineyard must be a place where the seeds of the Word are to be planted among the souls of men. It is a place where seeds take root and fruit is produced. The hired laborers are the laymen, teachers, pastors, parents, and individuals that go to work the vineyard of the souls of men. The day is the lifetime of each laborer. Many have given their whole lives from when they were very young believers to work the harvest of souls. Others have only come at the twilight of their life, in their old age to begin to work as the Lord hired them. So some labored all their life (all day). Others labored only the last days, at the 11th hour of their life. Everyone though was called to labor the vineyard.

When the Lord comes to the marketplace seeking workers will He find us standing there idle? When He asks us why we have been idle all day, all our life, will our answer be no one hired us? Have we not seen the need in the vineyard and sought out the landowner, the Lord that we might work with Him? Do we not know that He has already asked us to go work the vineyard?

If the King will pay the same wage to those who have labored in the heat of the day through all their lives as he will to the ones who only work one hour we may wonder what the wage is. With our understanding of the kingdom of God we must conclude that it is the eternal life we have been promised through belief in the King Jesus Christ. There is no indication that the all day laborers are more qualified for a wage than those who come the last hour. All receive a wage that is not decided by the number of hours worked nor their skill.

The question is; did they receive the wage of eternal life because they worked or did they work because they already had the gift of eternal life indicated by the invitation to work the fields. All those the landowner spoke to were invited to work the fields. The length of time of labor had nothing to do with the wage. The wage was already theirs, the wage of eternal life was given when the Father called. They went into the vineyards out of obedience to the landowner's request. They did not go to earn a wage. Yet it appears some felt they needed a greater reward, to have a higher position, to be first in the kingdom of God. The thoughts of being first as expressed by two disciples (Mark 10:35-45).

The parable is sandwiched between Matt 19:30 *"But many who are first will be last, and the last first"* and Matt 20:16 *"So the last will be first, and the first last. For many are called, but few chosen."*

We would wonder what this means if we did not begin with the context of the story (Matt 19:27–30). The parable is told in response to the disciple's question. Peter had just asked Jesus, we have left all we have and followed you, so what shall we receive? He was asking for wages just as those first called negotiated for wages with the landowner. Jesus tells Peter that the 12 disciples who have followed Him will sit on 12 thrones when He sits on His throne of glory. The 12 disciples will judge the 12 tribes of Israel. Then Jesus expanded this message to include all who have left their brothers, sisters, father, mother, children, or property for His name's sake will receive hundredfold, and will inherit eternal life.

This explains the wage. Every laborer receives eternal life and the love of God. All those other things that were left behind one should not worry about. Rather he should focus on the kingdom of God and let the Father take care of all things left behind. It is the King's prerogative to pay the same wage "eternal life" to the one who worked one hour as to the one who labored all day.

Many people resist coming into the kingdom because they feel no need for the righteousness of God instead relying on their own righteousness. Others come easily because they are broken and feel inadequate, knowing that they need a Savior. This is further explained in the next parable in Matt 21:31 where Jesus said that the tax collectors and harlots will enter the kingdom before the religious leaders. The broken humble heart is the first one willing to enter. Those who have much are the most resistant to a full dependency on the King.

In the context of the story the phrase *"many are called but few are chosen"* is in regards to laborers to work the field. Many are called to the kingdom of God. But few are specifically called or chosen by the King to go work the vineyard. Are we not told *"The harvest truly is plentiful, but the laborers are few. Therefore pray the Lord of the harvest to send out laborers into His harvest." (Matthew 9:37–38)*

We might ask of ourselves:

- Are we standing idle waiting to be hired? Would our excuse be that we have not been asked or is the truth that I have not heard and responded to the call to work by the King because our ears are closed?
- Would we really begrudge another laborer from the same wage of eternal life we receive even if they accept Jesus as Lord and Savior on their death bed? Rather should we not rejoice with them?
- Are we like the sons of Zebedee who desire a higher position in the kingdom?

8.2   Two types of citizens of the Kingdom

The Pharisees challenged Jesus by what authority he did all the miracles and His teachings. Rather than explaining where His authority came from, Jesus asked them if they thought John the Baptist baptism was from God or men. They did not answer Jesus because they feared the people. They hid their true thoughts by answering "we do not know". So then Jesus spoke to them in a parable about the kingdom of God.

This story is about a father, a vineyard owner, who had two sons (Matt 21:28-32). He came to his first son and said "*son, go work today in my vineyard*". At first this son rebelled against his father and disrespected him, saying "*I will not*". But afterwards this son regretted his rebellion toward his father's request and went to work the vineyard. The father also came to his second son and asked him to go work his vineyard. Now this son said to his father, "*I go sir*" but then he did not go. He faked his obedience and respect and then rebelled by not honoring his father's request.

Jesus then asked the Pharisees which man did the will of his father. They had to answer the first. He then turned the parable against them comparing the Pharisees to the tax collectors and prostitutes they so despised and judged. He compared the work of the Pharisees to the son who said he would work but did not and did not repent. They did not believe John the Baptist but the tax collectors and harlots believed. The Pharisees did not repent and believe John. Jesus challenged them by comparing them to the son who would not repent and work the vineyard. He challenged them by telling them that the tax collectors and prostitutes they despised would enter the kingdom before them. Before those who took pride in being the religious leaders.

This story again uses the illustration of the Father owning a vineyard and seeking laborers to work the vineyard. In this parable the prospective laborers are His own two sons. There is a difference in the son's face to face response to the Father and a difference in what they actually did later. The first son's response was rebellious. He even disrespected his Father to his face by saying no. But then he regretted what he said repented and went to work the vineyard. The second son pretended to be obedient to the fathers face, saying yes. But his true heart was revealed as he did not go into the vineyard to labor. Both sons were in rebellion against the Father, but one repented and the other did not.

Anyone who truly believes in Jesus Christ as the Creator, as the Savior and, as the King of the Kingdom will seek to do the will of the Father. He may rebel at first but conviction from the knowledge of the King will draw him towards repentance and obedience.

We can look around in our churches and see some standing idle as those in the market place in the previous parable. These same people may have heard the commands of Jesus to go work His vineyard. Did they say "yes sir I will go" but end up doing nothing to work in the kingdom. Hopefully it will not take a lifetime of rebellion before the motivation to serve the King changes their life.

It is possible that there are illegal aliens, pretenders, who have attempted to enter the kingdom without the seal of the Holy Spirit within the church. It is also possible that there are true citizens of the kingdom who are idle but have not heard the call of the Lord to work the vineyard. All they need is to hear is the words clearly spoken; come with me to work the vineyard. They may think they are not qualified to work the vineyard. They may not have the passion and compassion for others because they don't completely grasp the desire for love and oneness that the King has bestowed on His children.

Jesus uses this parable to address the rebellious son who made an appearance of being obedient but has rebelled and not repented. Does the example of a repentant son laboring in the vineyard compel us to examine ourselves and repent from our rebellion in not working the Father's vineyard? Conversely can our repentance, humility, and dedication to laboring in the vineyard inspire our brother to come alongside?

Which of these sons are we?

8.3   Evil tenants

In the previous parable Jesus is responding to the Pharisees hypocritical religious practices. He points out that their rebellion is against their God and their King. In that parable He uses the call of the Father to work His vineyard as a measure of their repentance and obedience to the will of the Father and ultimately examine their qualifications to enter the kingdom of God. But the Pharisee's did not yet understand their rebellion so he tells them another parable.

Again Jesus uses the illustration of a landowner having a vineyard. This landowner planted a vineyard and prepared for the fruit it would produce. He placed in the vineyard, at the disposal of the vinedressers, all they needed to prepare the vineyard and to harvest the fruit and the wine. He built a hedge of protection from the elements, a watchtower over the vineyard, and the winepress by which to produce the juice for the wine. Then He leased the vineyard to some vinedressers and went into a far country on a trip. He did not sell the vineyard to the vinedressers, he temporarily leased it to them.

When it was vintage time (the time of harvest) the landowner sent servants to the vineyard to receive some of its fruit from the vinedressers. But the vinedressers beat one of the landowner's servants, killed one, and stoned another. The landowner sent more servants to receive some of the fruit. Again the vinedressers did the same to these servants. Finally the landowner sent His son to them, saying surely they will respect my son. But when the vinedressers saw the son, they plotted against him reasoning among themselves that if we kill the son, the only heir, the vineyard then will be ours. So they killed the landowner's son (Matt 21:33-46).

When Jesus finished telling the parable He asked the Pharisees what the landowner would do when he returned. The Pharisees prescribed this judgement; the landowner will destroy those wicked men "miserably" and give the vineyard to other vinedressers who will give the fruits to the landowner.

Jesus responded by quoting from Psa 118:22-24, scriptures which they purported to know. This scripture states that the stone which the builders rejected has become the chief cornerstone according to the Lord's doing and that there is great rejoicing in it. The Pharisees had not grasped that they represented the son who said he would work the vineyard but did not in the previous parable. This parable was more direct. The stone the builders (the Jews, the Pharisees) rejected had become the chief cornerstone, speaking of Himself. Jesus told them *"therefore the kingdom of God will be taken away from you and given to a nation bearing the fruits of it"*.

This the chief priests and Pharisees understood. They realized Jesus was talking about them. They had rejected the Kings servants, the prophets. They had killed some of them. But even now after hearing this parable they continued to live out what was described in the parable as they planned to kill the Son of the owner of the vineyard, Jesus Christ.

The time was at hand when the Father, the landowner, had sent His son Jesus. But the vinedressers left in charge, the religious leaders and Pharisees were not interested in the fruits of the vine. They only wanted to own the vineyard for themselves. This was a prophecy of what they were about to do. They would kill the Son of God. They wanted to be king, to own the land, to be in charge. However, the landowner would judge them for their deeds. They prescribed their own judgement through this conversation and Jesus spoke the judgement back to them right there and then. They had rejected the stone, the Messiah of whom it was prophesied was to come. But that stone they rejected would become the chief cornerstone, the cornerstone of the church the King was going to build. The building of the kingdom would be taken away from them and given to another nation, the Gentiles.

They had known the truths of God but had not used them to prepare for the building of the kingdom. They had not taught the people and brought to them to the truths given to them. Throughout history the Jews had only been interested in themselves. So the judgement they prescribed for the tenants was to themselves when they responded to Jesus question. The judgement that the vineyard was to be taken away from them and given to a nation that would invest in the souls that are in the vineyard. It was given to the Gentiles.

Once again in order to describe the kingdom of God Jesus used a; landowner, a vineyard, and hired servants to work the vineyard. But in this case He added the son of the landowner, the heir. He described a vineyard which the owner had prepared to produce the desired fruit. A vineyard for which the workers had been given all the tools necessary to work and bring in its harvest. All had been made ready for the hired servants to work the vineyard before the landowner went off to a faraway land.

He planted a hedge around the vineyard. A hedge to protect the vineyard from winds, to provide nitrogen to the soils, to protect it from intruders. A hedge to be an indicator of the health of the vineyard to alert the servants of insects about to invade the vineyard.

The landowner placed a watchtower above the vineyard. A place from which the vinedressers could oversee the whole vineyard. They could see where the vineyard needed more water. Places where the vines needed pruning. Places where the grapes ripened earlier. They could also see if there was an intruder who had come in to steal the crop. This position of oversight tells of a position where some of the servants are to act as overseers of the vineyard as they nurture the crop and protect the crop. They had been given prophets to oversee Israel. In our time we would liken this position of oversight as the task of the pastor, elders, deacons of the church, and the father of a family. We could liken the tower as the word of God upon which the overseer stands and watches over the vineyard.

The landowner also gave them a winepress by which they could reap the harvest. They could squeeze the grapes into grape juice let it ferment and make wine. Wine which could be given to merchants and sold into the world. We could liken this to the lives of believers who are squeezed through trials that their faith might be found genuine (1 Pet 1:6–7). Who then export the fruit of the Spirit that the world might taste of it and desire to find its source.

This parable is a judgement against the Pharisees the religious leaders of the Children of Israel. They were given the vineyard of their own children to work the harvest. They were to be a testimony to the vineyard of the world. They were given all the necessary items from which to produce fruit. They had the laws of Moses, they had the Prophets, and they had seen God care for them over and over again. They had the words of the prophets speaking in anticipation of the returning King. But throughout history they had beaten, stoned, and killed the prophets God had sent them. They had not nurtured the vineyard and harvested its fruits.

This parable can also be a judgement against the church member and religious leaders of today. Those who persecute the pastor and destroy his life. Those with stiff necks who will not incline their ears to hear what the Spirit says to the churches. Those who have been given all the tools to work the vineyard of souls but are only interested in owning the buildings and organizations for themselves.

You and I are now in this position of having all the tools necessary to work the vineyard of the Father. We are that nation, you and I are a special people, to whom has been given the Gospel of the Kingdom that we might proclaim it. We have the Word of God and the testimonies of the disciples. More than that we have been sent the Holy Spirit to help us. We must now ask ourselves, you and me individually, not our pastors and teachers, if we want to be like the Pharisees and do nothing with what we have been given or to work the vineyard of souls and bring the harvest to the King. Since the time of Jesus many nations have been given the Gospel and for a time were faithful to work the vineyards of the world. But as they forgot over time God moved the labor to other nations who rose up to work the vineyard and bring forth its fruits. Will you and I as individuals go into the vineyard and work the harvest?

This parable is not about us as the original vinedressers, but we must look at it as having received the vineyard after it was taken away from the children of Israel, we are now responsible to work it.

8.4   Wise and foolish builders

Now we will look at two parables that are very personal and individual to each one of us. They point directly at what truth resides in our hearts.

The first parable is meant for us to examine our hearts and ask ourselves what we treasure. To ask if we are spending time investing in things that are futile and will pass away. To know for sure that we belong to the kingdom of God. That we are citizens of the kingdom. That the King knows us.

But before this parable is told Jesus first says something that is very challenging to us (Matt 7:21-23). He tells us that not everyone who calls Him, "Lord, Lord" will enter the kingdom of heaven. This should cause us to examine ourselves. Incline your ears to this; Jesus said that I can call Him Lord yet I might not be able to enter the kingdom of heaven. At the time of judgement many will say to the King; have we not prophesied, or taught in your name? This is not just a few but many. Some will even say we cast out demons in your name. We have done wonders in your name.

Scary thought, that we who have believed that we will someday enter the kingdom of heaven might be excluded because the Lord does not know us. Today one of us might say it this way; I went to church each week, I tithed faithfully, I taught Sunday school for 20 years, I even baptized some. Could it be that even through this labor which I thought was for Him I might hear those dreadful words; "I never knew you; depart from Me, you who practice lawlessness?

I could say that I know the president of the United States. I know his name. I know his values and his goals. I have listened to his speeches and have even gone to a political rally where he shook my hand. But could I say that the president knows me? Could it be that we have attended church, heard the word from the pulpit and yet do not know if the Lord knows us?

This parable points at the heart of the individual. His love for the Lord. His surrender and work to the will of the Father. Evidenced by where the individual spends his time, in what he invests, and on what he builds.

The key question that emerges from this passage is the critical determination for entry; does the Lord know me. Entry has nothing to do with me working the vineyards but whether or not the Lord knows me.

The works do not open the door to the kingdom. It is the relationship with Jesus Christ that opens the door.

How then can I determine if the Lord knows me? There is one scripture that addresses this directly *"if anyone loves God, this one is known by Him"* (1 Cor 8:3). The next obvious question would be; do I REALLY love God. It is the first love commandment given; that we should love the Lord our God with all our heart, soul, mind, and strength (Luke 10:27). Do I love the Lord above all else, above all self, with all my heart, my soul, my mind, and my strength. This question deserves serious self-examination and seeking.

The second question, which follows from the first, is measured in our behaviors. Jesus said; if you love me keep my commandments (John 14:15). This is a response out of love, an outcome of the commandment that we must love Him. It is not to be confused with works that we might think we must do in order to be made known. Works like attending church, tithing, teaching, etc. It is a measuring stick by which we can examine our love for Him. We do not keep His commandments to acquire love for Him, rather because we love Him we keep His commandments. We love Him because He first loved us (1 John 4:19).

If our love for Him produces a desire to keep His commandments and to do His will then we know that we know Him (1 John 2:3–5). That is what Jesus is referring to when he states; not everyone who says "Lord, Lord" shall enter the kingdom of heaven, BUT he who does the will of my Father in heaven will enter the kingdom of heaven. It is a response out of love for Him that results in an individual desiring to keep His commands and do His will. Love must be sincere.

Now to this parable.

After this challenge from the criteria for entry into the kingdom being dependent on the King knowing us Jesus tells a parable of the builders of a house (Matt 7:24-27). The emphasis is on the foundation upon which a house is built *"built on the foundation of the apostles and prophets, Jesus Christ Himself being the chief cornerstone"* (Eph 2:19-22)

He tells us that the person who hears Jesus words and does them is like a wise man who builds his house on the rock. The foundation upon which the house is built is Jesus Christ. The tools and the method of building is by adhering to the words that Jesus spoke. Jesus is the architect of the house. Then when the winds, the rain, the floods come the house stands and does not fall.

On the other hand the person who hears the words of Jesus and does not do them is like a man who builds his house on sand. This man chooses to build the house with his own plans, with his own tools. He ignores the words of Jesus and builds according to his own desires. This man is the architect of his own house. In not heeding the words of Jesus this house is not built upon the rock but on sand. When the winds, the rain, the floods come that house falls.

The one who builds his house on his own ideas of teaching, preaching, healing, even casting out demons in the name of Jesus is building his house on the sand. But he who builds on the pure words of Jesus is building his house upon the rock. The one on the sand attempts to produce fruit when, and where he feels it needs to be produced – trying to achieve. The one on the rock produces fruit when the Creator calls him to produce fruit in the season determined by the Creator (Psa 1:2-3).. True ministry is received not achieved. The one building on the rock has big ears that listen to the Spirit. The one building on the sand has deaf ears that do not hear the Spirit.

It is not the outward work that identifies the individual with the kingdom of God. It is the condition of the inward heart.

- What will the Lord say to me when I stand before Him, will He say He does not know me? Do I truly love Him?
- Who sits on the throne of my heart? Does the King really rule on the throne of my heart, the land He purchased with His blood?

- Am I building my house on the foundation of the apostles with Jesus Christ as the cornerstone according to the pure words of Jesus rather than the desires of my flesh?

8.5   Characteristic of an unmerciful servant

One of the problems we face is that others hurt us. They may forget to do something that is important to us. They may say something about us or about someone we love that hurts us. They may even steal from us or strike us. Then when they repent and ask us to forgive them it is hard for us to forgive. It is even harder for us to forget what they have done to us and then love them.

Peter, one of the Apostles, asked this question of Jesus (Matt 18:21-22). Lord, how often shall my brother sin against me, and I forgive him? As he asked, Peter put the number 7 times on it thinking it was a large number and would be an example of the offended brother showing great grace. After all how can we believe that the offending person really repented if he repeats the offense 7 times and then repeats it once again? Jesus response challenges us. He said not just 7 times but 70 times seven. The meaning of this is that we forgive the offending person every time he repents from his offence.   There is no end to the number of times we forgive the offender.

Jesus explains this principle a bit more with a parable about the kingdom of Heaven (God) in (Matt 18:23-35).

The kingdom of heaven is like a certain king who wanted to settle accounts with his servants. As he was settling his accounts one servant was brought to him who owed him 10,000 talents (that is 1 Million pounds of gold). The servant was not able to pay so the master gave the command that he be sold, with his wife and their children and all his possessions. The servant fell down before the master and begged him to have patience with him. He said "I will pay you all". The master was moved with compassion, released him, and unbelievably forgave him this irreconcilable great debt. He no longer owed the master anything. Nothing. He was debt free from a debt he could never have paid.

But the servant went out and found a fellow servant that owed him 100 days wages. He took the man by the throat and said *"pay me what you owe"*! His fellow servant fell down at his feet and begged him saying *"have patience with me and I will pay you all"*. But the servant did not have patience and threw his fellow servant in prison. When the master found out what the servant had done to his fellow servant he called him to confront him. You wicked servant, he said. I forgave you so great a debt because you begged me. Should you not have also had compassion on your fellow servant just as I had pity on you? So the master gave this evil servant over to be tortured until he should pay all that was due.

Jesus gives a short but very important explanation of the parable to us about forgiveness when he states; *"So My heavenly Father also will do to you if each of you, from his heart, does not forgive his brother his trespasses"* (Matt 18:35)

We all have been forgiven a debt we cannot pay. Paid by the Father by sending His own Son, paid by Jesus Christ with His own blood. There is no sacrifice, no offering, nor a count of the number of sacrifices, offerings, or merit that sum up sufficiently to pay the debt of sin and rebellion we all have. But the Father through the Son has offered forgiveness through Jesus Christ. If we just accept the gift of the sacrifice of His Son and believe in Him our debt is erased.

If we don't forgive others we have not grasped the magnitude of the gift given by the Father and the Son. We have not truly accepted the free gift of forgiveness from the Father in our hearts. We have not understood how great His love and compassion is towards us. As we have been forgiven such a great debt God, the Father, will throw us into outer darkness if we do not forgive anyone and everyone who needs our forgiveness. Not just words of forgiveness. Not just actions of forgiveness. Jesus says it must come from our very hearts! We must completely forgive so that we do not even have thoughts of unforgiveness within our hearts!

The importance of forgiveness is expressed in our response to the Lord's Prayer (Matt 6:9-15). We ask for forgiveness from the Father in this prayer and ask Him to forgive us as we forgive those who trespass against us. But we must read on after the Lord's Prayer in (Matt 6:14-15). Jesus explains that forgiveness from the Father is conditional on our forgiveness of others. That can only happen if it is from our hearts. If His love resides within us we will be able to forgive those who trespass against us from the depths of our heart.

We tend to limit this idea of forgiveness to each event as it occurs. We consider that we must forgive each time someone trespasses against us; the past sin. We may go even further and realize that we should forgive immediately when the trespass occurs and not hold on to it; the present sin. But we should note that by Jesus death on the cross He forgave our sins past, present, and future. When we forgive we should have the attitude that we forgive our spouses, our neighbors not just for sins in the past or present but in advance of their future trespasses against us. God's forgiveness for us was; I forgive you all things you have done in the past, I forgive you for that which you did just now, AND I forgive you in advance for any trespass you will commit against me in the future. He has already forgiven us those sins which we will commit against Him tomorrow. That is the level of forgiveness we must have towards our brethren and our neighbors.

If we are the one forgiven it is not a license to go out and sin again expecting an unending well of forgiveness. The servant who was forgiven such a great debt pleaded with his master but did not repent in his heart. He had no need for the money from his fellow servant. He continued his practice of serving himself. That which got him into such a great debt in the first place.

8.6   Summary of the vineyard and its laborers

Our Father has a vineyard of souls, the world, into which He desires to send us, the laborers. There is much work to be done. We as adopted sons of the Father have been asked to go and tend to the souls that are in the body of Christ and export the fruit of the Spirit into world. It is not of our works but hearing His call and doing His will on the basis of Him ruling in the kingdom of our hearts.

We must hear the pure words of Jesus and build according to His plan, not ours. We must check our hearts to see if we truly love Him and so love our fellow servants.

9   Celebration of the King

A time is coming when this part of the story will be completed. The part
of the story of the King building of the kingdom of God. It will finish with
a very large celebration put on by the Father of the King. Many guests
are invited. But many will ignore the invitation. Some will desire to go to
the celebration but because they have not prepared they will miss the
King when He comes. The King has promised to come again to receive
His bride (the believers called the church) and take them to this great
supper, the marriage feast of the Lamb.

We will look at two parables of Jesus that describe the end of the
building of the Kingdom of God; the wedding feast, and the watchful and
foolish virgins.

These two parables are directed at us individually.   Will we accept the
invitation to the wedding feast? Will we be found ever watchful for the
coming of the King?

9.1   A celebration for the King – The wedding feast

Jesus had been observing how the Jews behaved at a feast. They would
invite their friends and relatives. The invited guests would strive for the
best place at the table that would give them honor. Honor higher than
those seated at lesser positions. Later those who had been invited would
also set up a feast reciprocating with invitations to their friends and
relatives. It was all fabricated to build up self with honor between men in
the community. It was a competition between friends and relatives for
the best place and the greatest honor. Pride drove their behavior.

Jesus told them that an invitation to a friend, a brother, a relative or your
rich neighbor will result in them wanting to pay you back by inviting you
to their house for a feast. Jesus advised them; rather than inviting those
who can repay you; invite the poor, the lame, and the blind who cannot
repay you for your goodness. Then you will be blessed at the time of the
resurrection of the just. (Luke 14:12-14). This advice is a call to give up
the self-edification that we desire at the present.

Then Jesus told a parable of the kingdom of God illustrating it through a parable of a man giving a great supper (Luke 14:15–24). There was a man who planned a great supper and invited many guests. When the time came for the supper and all the preparations were made he sent out his servants to say to those invited *"come for all things are now ready"*. But those invited began to make excuses. One said I have bought a piece of ground and must go and see it – please excuse me. Another said I have bought five yoke of oxen and am going to test them – please excuse me. Still another said I have married a wife and therefore cannot come. So the servant went back to the man who had planned the great supper and told him these things. The master of the house was very angry and told his servant to go out into the streets and alleys of the city. Invite the poor, the lame, and the blind. The servant did as he was told and reported to the master of the house that it had been done. Yet there was room at the feast table. Then the master sent the servant out the highways and the hedge rows to call everyone to come saying *"that my house may be filled"*. The master of the house said that none of those who had been first invited and refused to come would taste of the masters supper.

This story illustrates the giving of an invitation to come and celebrate with the Father and His Son, the wedding feast of the King when Jesus presents the kingdom of God to the Father. The Jews refused the invitation so the Father sent His servant out to give the invitation everywhere, the cities, the highways, the fields, to the Gentiles. An invitation to all the world, to every tribe and nation to join the kingdom of God.

Everyone who has heard the Gospel has received an invitation. But so many, oh so many refuse to come because of their treasures in this world. Their lands, their oxen, and their wives. They value them more than they value the invitation from the King of kings. This is not just any feast. This is the feast of the marriage supper of the Lamb of God, the King, Jesus Christ, the Son of God.

The people who reject the invitation remain in rebellion against the King as they will not let Him rule in their hearts. They treasure the temporary satisfactions that this world offers. The truth is they want to rule over their lives and be their own king just as the deceiver taught their father and mother in the Garden of Eden. They have chosen as their father the deceiver.

But the poor, the lame, the blind are without earthly treasures. They have none. They are not filled by the desires of this world and so they more easily accept the invitation of the Father's servants. But even these may not accept if they have other gods that they have made for themselves. The King has sent His servants to the whole world to invite all peoples to His Son's wedding feast. To all tribes and tongues. To the unreached. To those who have not heard the invitation. That His house might be filled.

Those who will come to the wedding banquet at the end of time; the wife, or bride, has made herself ready for the wedding feast. She is dressed in fine linen, the finest clothes available. Her clothes are clean, without spot or wrinkle cleansed from sin by the sacrifice of the King (Rev 19:6-9). They have been washed in the blood of the Lamb. The bride has chosen keep her clothing clean and pure by doing only the will of the Father. Her clothes shine, they are bright and her life is such that the light of the world, the King, shines through her. The clothes of fine linen she wears are made up of righteous deeds as she exports the fruit of the Spirit; love, joy, peace, longsuffering, kindness, goodness, faithfulness, gentleness, and self-control (Gal 5:22).

But how did the bride wash her clothes to make them so bright and clean? Did she do it by her will, her dedication, and her own effort?

No, the bridegroom, the King Himself, has provided the means by which she would become clean. The King loved the church so much He gave Himself for her. So that He might set His bride apart, clean and pure cleansing her and washing her by His Words. All this so that He might present her to Himself without spot or wrinkle, a glorious bride worthy of a King. Holy and without blemish (Eph 5:25-27).

> *Eph 5:25–27 25 Husbands, love your wives, just as Christ also loved the church and gave Himself for her, 26 that He might sanctify and cleanse her with the washing of water by the word, 27 that He might present her to Himself a glorious church, not having spot or wrinkle or any such thing, but that she should be holy and without blemish.*

The King cleansed her and set her aside for Himself by washing her with the water of the Word. The living water of the Holy Spirit and the Word of the Father given through Jesus to the church. The church which is the Kingdom of God and the bride of Christ.

If we plan to be at the wedding feast we must be there clean and pure. We must let the Word of God flow through our minds and hearts to clean us. As we let the Word flow through us our King will wash our hearts to be pure and clean. As we are washed clean no darkness will remain in our hearts. Then the King can shine through us for all the world to see His glory.

9.2   The watchful and foolish virgins

In the previous parable we finish with; the believers who are the church, the bride, has made herself ready for the coming wedding feast. It is worth taking a look at how people might make themselves ready. Especially since this is talking about us. We who desire to enter the kingdom of God and who desire to be with the King throughout eternity. Jesus told us a parable about the ones who are anticipating the coming bridegroom of the kingdom of God.

During the time of Jesus the culture was that when a marriage was set the bridegroom would go to prepare a place, a house to live in with his future wife. While he was off preparing the house the bride was preparing herself. It was very important for the bride to be always ready.

Always dressed in her finest clothes for she did not know when the bridegroom would return and call for her.

Jesus told a story about 10 virgins who took their lamps and went out to meet the bridegroom when the unscheduled call came. These were lamps that used oil to fuel the wick which then burned to give light. Five of the virgins took extra oil with them. Five others did not take oil with their lamps. As in the Jewish tradition the bridegroom did not come immediately. So all of the virgins slept while they were waiting. But at midnight a cry came *"behold the bridegroom is coming; go out to meet him"*. When the virgins heard the cry they got up and trimmed their lamps to provide more light. They adjusted the wick and added oil so that the lamps would burn more brightly. But the foolish virgins who did not bring oil asked the five wise virgins for some of their oil. But the five wise virgins did not give of their oil lest their own lamps also go out. The five wise virgins told the foolish virgins to go out and buy oil from those who sell oil. But as they went out to buy the bridegroom came. Those who were ready went with him to the wedding and the door was shut. When the foolish virgins came to the house they cried out *"Lord open to us"*. But the bridegroom said *"I do not know you"*. (Matt 25:1-13)

Jesus tells this story and then gives the instruction to watch and be ready because we do not know the day or the hour in which the Son of Man is coming". This story is part of a long dissertation that Jesus gives in response to the disciples question; when will these things be, and what will be the signs of your coming at the end of the age beginning in (Matt 24:3). It is in the timeline of the last days and is a reflection of the condition of those who are waiting for the rapture. Some are standing fast being watchful. Others are not ready.

This should be one of those wake up stories for us. If our desire is to go with the Son of Man, the bridegroom, to the wedding feast will He come and find us watching with our lamps giving out light? Or will our hearts be found without oil? Will we try to enter His house after the door is shut but find that it is too late?

Jesus said He is the light of the world (John 8:12) and as long as Jesus was in the world He was that light (John 9:5). Today Jesus is not in the world but His Spirit lives within us. So then He is still the light of the world but from inside our hearts, inside the lamp of our souls, we are the light of the world (Matt 5:14). The oil that feeds the light is the Spirit. Those that sell the oil are the teachers of the Word and preachers of the kingdom of God.

No one knows when the Son of Man will return. If we say; I will think about it and maybe I will accept Jesus Christ the King's invitation tomorrow we may miss the coming of the bridegroom. If we wait we are just like those invited to the feast that were more interested in their fields, livestock, and wives in the parable of the wedding feast.

We must be always watching and waiting for we do not know the time He will come. Jesus told us that we must have our waist girded and our lamps burning. We must be like men who wait for their master when he knocks that they may open to him immediately. For no one knows when he will return. The Son of Man, the King is coming at an hour, a time, when we do not expect (Luke 12:35-48). If we are apathetic about feeding our hearts with the Word of God, our hearts will be empty of the oil that gives light at His coming. If our hearts do not have the Spirit within it, there is not oil and no light. We do not have the seal of the Spirit guaranteeing entry into the Kingdom.

We have been warned not to falter or fade but hold fast and keep our lights burning and our waist girded with the belt of truth of the Word. We must have our lamps burning, giving off the light of the Spirit within us into the darkness of the world. Lamps that are lit with the oil of the Holy Spirit.

10   The Citizens responsibilities - Stewards of Souls

We now come to the last parable of this study. It is also the last parable Jesus told to the disciples when they asked Him when the end of time would be and what would be the signs of His coming. It is part of the timeline of the events of the end. This parable tells us of the accounting the King will require of each citizen's investment during His absence.

Jesus begins this parable with the words "the kingdom of heaven is like" indicating it will illustrate something about the kingdom of heaven, the kingdom of God, that He wants us to know. This particular parable uses the illustration of investing and money to describe stewardship of what the King values in the kingdom of God. Because this parable utilizes talents (Matt 25:14-30) and minas (Luke 19:9-27) in its illustration this parable has most often been used to teach about the believer's stewardship of money and wealth. In some cases this parable has been used to teach good stewardship of an individual's spiritual gifts. To be sure we must be stewards of all the Lord has given to us, but throughout this study we have come to understand that the kingdom of God is about the souls of men. So then this parable is about the souls of men and how we the citizens of the kingdom have cared for and invested in the souls entrusted to us.

Given what we already know, we will however, walk through an assessment of the meaning of the goods belonging to the nobleman, the talent and mina and what the implications are to the servant.

If we are the stewards and the nobleman is coming back to see what we have done with the goods he left in our charge then we need to know what those goods are. We can't be good stewards if we don't understand the values of the King and the meaning of "talents" or "minas" he left in our charge.

We have some questions about this parable;
1) What is a talent and what is a mina?
    1) Is the intent of this parable to literally focus on the stewardship of money and how or where we invest our money, as in tithing to the church?

2) Could a talent or mina be a reference person's abilities or spiritual gifts instead of money?

3) Are the parables a stewardship question that refers to a broader view of how we manage all the material things that God has given us; my job, my personal investments, my time, my tithing, my home, my car, etc?

Or

4) Was Jesus using money and our understanding of money management to illustrate investing in something of value to the King on earth that retains its value in the kingdom of heaven, the souls of men?

2) What was the investment and how was the investment to be made by the faithful servants?

1) Did these servants speculate in schemes, stock markets or other growth areas?

2) Did these servants somehow expand the business by shrewd business dealings?

Or

3) Did the servants understand what the master valued and so expended their time and effort into carrying out the master's commands of growing the kingdom of God by multiplying souls?

3) What does it mean that the unfaithful servant buried or hid the master's talent?

1) He says he was afraid, but was he really afraid of losing the masters talent or was he afraid of peer criticisms?

2) When he buried or hid the talent did he literally bury money keeping it to himself or was he just slothful in doing nothing to grow the kingdom of God with what that which had been given to him?

3) Was it fear, or was it that he really did not care about the talent nor the master?

The Context

Jesus placed two parables describing the kingdom of heaven right in the midst of His response to the Apostles question *"Tell us, when will these things be, and what will be the sign of your coming and of the close of the age?* Jesus responds with a speech that spans Matt 24:4 to Matt 25:46.

We have to put this parable in the context and ask; why are The Parable of the Ten Virgins and the Parable of the Talents placed in the context and timeline of this discussion? The content and the purpose of these parables must be related to His response to the Apostles in explaining the events that lead up to end of time.

The content and theme of Jesus response in Matt 24 through Matt 25 follows this order:

The condition of the nations and people on the earth

The Great Tribulation

Jesus return as the conquering King

The sign of His imminent coming, the parable of the fig tree (Mat 24:32–35)

The condition of man will be like those at the time of Noah

The rapture described, some taken some left

<u>Illustration of the watchful and the unfaithful servant (Matt 24:45-51)</u>

Parable of wise and foolish virgins (Matt 25:1-13)

Parable of the talents (Matt 25:14-30)

<u>The final judgment</u>

From this sequence we see that the parable of the wise and foolish virgins and the parable of the talents are sandwiched between a comparison of the watchful and unfaithful servants surprised by the return of their master and the final judgment of man. Thus the parable of the talents clearly falls into the context of the end of time and judgments passed on to man.

Just before the parable of the wise and foolish virgins, Jesus provides a comparison of a faithful to an unfaithful servant. A comparison of what the servants did with what the master had put in their charge and what the master would do when he returned for an accounting of what they are doing when he returns.

> *"Who then is a faithful and wise servant, whom <u>his master made ruler over his household, to give them food in due season</u>? Blessed is that servant whom his master, when he comes, will find so doing. Assuredly, I say to you that he will make him ruler over all his goods. But if that evil servant says in his heart, 'My master is delaying his coming,' and begins to beat his fellow servants, and to eat and drink with the drunkards, the master of that servant will come on a day when he is not looking for him and at an hour that he is not aware of, and will cut him in two and appoint him his portion with the hypocrites. There shall be weeping and gnashing of teeth (Matt 24:45–51).*

This illustration highlights that there is an accounting coming from the master of the household when he returns. It is clear the servants did not know when the master would return otherwise they would make sure they were engaging in the masters business at the time of his return.

Then in the discussion that follows the parable of the talents Jesus describes His return and His final judgment illustrating this with the separation of the sheep from the goats. Similar to the parables describing the separation of the wheat from the tares and the good fish from the bad at the end of time.

In Luke, the text prior to the parable of the minas ends with a statement by Jesus *"for the Son of Man has come to seek and to save that which was lost"* and then is linked to the parable of the minas with the statement *"Now as they heard these things, He spoke another parable"*. This context draws you away from the idea that the parable of the talents/minas is talking about money, possessions, tithing, and spiritual gifts as the primary topic. It draws you back towards that for which Jesus came, the lost. It fits with the focus on the souls of men from all the other parables regarding the kingdom of God.

Though money and physical and spiritual gifts may be useful tools to attaining the objective, *"to save that which was lost"*, they are not the talent or the mina themselves.

The talents did not add to the servants abilities, <u>they already had sufficient abilities</u> to perform the task they were given. They already had all the spiritual gifts needed to care for the goods left in their care.

> *Matt 25:15 And to one he gave five talents, to another two, and to another one, to each <u>according to his own ability</u>; and immediately he went on a journey.*

So the context points us to focus on the same primary objective Jesus gave in His commandment to His citizens; go and make disciples of all nations. The talents are neither material possessions nor spiritual gifts. They are souls.

The context before the parable provides the idea of investment in the household of the Master through providing food. The only "food" we have to give to the household of the kingdom of God is the food of the Gospel. The living water, the bread of life who is Jesus Christ.

> *Mat 24:45-46 "Who then is a faithful and wise servant, whom his master made ruler over his household, <u>to give them food in due season?</u> Blessed is that servant whom his master, when he comes, will find so doing.*

That faithful servant, who was made head of the household, feeds those within the household with the food of the word of God. He is faithful, being found carrying out the work of feeding the household when the master returns. Those in the household would be the sheep of the shepherd, the fellow believers and citizens. This faithful servant is found teaching the things of the kingdom of God to faithful men who will be able to teach others also (2 Tim2:2) upon the masters return.

I would submit that the parable of the faithful and wise servant, of the wise and foolish virgins, and the parable of the talents represent the characteristics of men at the time of Jesus return. The parable of the faithful servant is about being faithful in feeding the citizens of the kingdom with the word of God. The subject of the parable of the wise and foolish virgins is about the preparedness and watchfulness of the individual's own heart in being prepared for the bridegroom's return. The parable of the talents is about the investments the individual is making or has made in that which is of value to our Lord, the souls of men. **So then, a talent or a mina represents a soul put in our lives in to which we are expected to invest.** I believe this understanding is critical to what the church will do with our remaining time.

The following discussion provides arguments that talents and minas represent souls – not money, not tithing, and not physical or spiritual gifts.

The Master or Nobleman

We can safely say that the lord in the parable of the talents and the nobleman in the parable of the minas is the Lord Jesus Christ Himself. So that being true what kind of light does that shed on the focus that is placed on the talents and minas of these two parables?

There are certainly a lot of parallels between the Lord Jesus and the nobleman of these parables. The lord or nobleman goes to a faraway land for a time leaving his servants in charge of his assets. Just so Jesus went to the Father and left His followers in charge. The lord or nobleman returns after a time and tests his servants on what they did with that put under their charge. Just so Jesus said He will return to judge His servants for their works.

If the lord or nobleman represents Jesus then how can the talents and minas represent money, tithes, physical gifts, or even spiritual gifts? Did Jesus leave his vineyards to the Apostles to care for? Did Jesus leave a bank account that He expected the Apostles to multiply on His return? No, Jesus had no physical possessions on this Earth. He left nothing of monetary value for someone to benefit from or to care for.

You would expect that prior to the lord or nobleman departure he himself would have been investing in the very thing, his goods, he expected his servants to care for. Jesus whole life here on Earth was about coming to *"seek and save that which was lost"* and preaching the kingdom of God. He valued the lost souls of men. So much so He paid a great price, the price of a pure lamb to purchase the souls of men. He had no investments in earthly things. The Son of man even had no place to lay his head (Matt 8:20).

The name of the lord or nobleman, Jesus Christ, then is sufficient to define what the subject of these parables is. On this basis alone the talents and minas can only represent souls. The question is; how well did the servants invest in the souls put in their charge. The question to us is; are we investing in the souls God has entrusted to us?

The Subject Material (talent or mina)

To help understand the thought process of the people of the day when a talent or mina term was used, we include the definitions:

<u>In Matthew the word "talent" is used</u>

Talent:= *Talanton*

- Root Word: From a presumed derivative of the original form of *tlao*
    - To carry some burden
    - To bear, endure the rigor of a thing, ones conduct
1) the scale of a balance, a balance, a pair of scales
2) that which is weighed, a talent
   a) a weight varying in different places and times
   b) a sum of money weighing a talent and varying in different states and according to the changes in the laws regulating currency
      i) the Attic talent was equal to 60 Attic minae or 6000 drachmae
      ii) a talent of silver in Israel weighed about 100 pounds (45 kg)
      iii) a talent of gold in Israel weighed about 200 pounds (91 kg

<u>In Luke the word "minas" is used</u>

Mna:= pound

- Hebrew: mna: to appoint, mark out, count, etc.
- Latin mina
1) In the OT a weight, and an imaginary coin or money of account, equal to 100 shekels [1 Kings 10:17, 2 Chr 9:16]
2) In Attic a weight and sum of money equal to 100 draqchmae
   1) in the OT, a weight of 300 shekels was one pound

2) In the NT, a weight and sum of money equal to 100 drachmae, one talent was 100 pounds, a pound equaled 10 1/3 oz. (300 gm)

The people of Jesus time would have recognized the talent as a measure, a collection, or a weight of money not as an individual coin. It was an imaginary quantity of money measured by weight.

There is another aspect to the word talent that comes from the root word meaning to bear something as in a burden, part of a stewards life. A steward carries the burden of a task and makes decisions based on the balance of what information is before him.

It is also not likely that the talents or minas refer to a physical skill or a spiritual ability. The definitions of the talent and mina don't relate to these at all. In addition the parable of the talents says the talents were distributed to each one according to their abilities. The implication is they already had all the physical and spiritual abilities to care for the talents entrusted into their care.

There is one aspect of the parables that correlates a characteristic of money to the minas and talents. They have the ability to be multipliers. Money properly invested can generate more money. This is also the characteristic of a soul saved by grace. A soul properly invested in multiplies as a witness to bring other souls to Christ.

In Luke the faithful servants traded in the minas and it is stated that *"your mina has earned ten minas"* and *"your mina has earned five minas"*. The minas earned more minas, not the servant himself. These souls, the faithful servants invested in brought more souls into the kingdom of God.

In Matthew the servant who received 5 talents went and traded with them. Trading with these talents (souls) paints a picture of the servant walking with these souls, instructing them as they walked gathering souls using the dragnet of the kingdom of God. Giving and receiving as they break the word of God. What took place was a feeding of the souls put in the servants charge and the training of those souls in the fishing for more souls.

This is in alignment with Paul giving Timothy the instruction to invest in faithful men who are able to teach others also (2 Tim 2:2).

The determining question is; what is of value to the master and in the kingdom of heaven. It is souls.

Stewardship

Is the parable about stewardship? Yes, stewardship is the primary activity being discussed in the parable. The two faithful servants were active in taking care of the talents whereas the slothful servant was idle. The two faithful servants worked and invested their time taking care of and multiplying their master's assets. The slothful servant was lazy, at best only keeping the master's assets safe.

The context of the illustration of the faithful and wise servant who is feeding the household when the master returns places the focus of this parable on stewardship of that which the master has put into the servants hands. Feeding the souls put into his charge with the word of God.

One can be a good steward of his tithing and the use of his abilities but there is no indication that giving or tithing to the church or a performing a good work has any connection to these parables of the talents and minas. Since tithing was a well-known characteristic of a righteous man of Jesus day you would think it would be directly mentioned in the text if that were what it was about. The flavor of the parable does not even hint at the practice of giving a percentage or of a first fruit. No percentage of the talents was "given" to the lord or nobleman when he was gone but rather <u>all</u> the talents were under the steward's management and <u>all</u> were returned to the lord upon his return. Though tithing is an expected practice it is not purpose of this parable.

Would not that which is of value to the master, be measured by the master's viewpoint and not man's viewpoint? The masters statement to do business with the minas until he returns is consistent with the departing command given by Jesus *"Go therefore and make disciples of all the nations, baptizing them in the name of the Father and of the Son and of the Holy Spirit, teaching them to observe all things that I have commanded you"* (Matt 28:19–20). Jesus last instruction to us is to make disciples i.e. invest in the souls of men so that they would understand and follow all things Jesus commanded us through the Gospels. Do business with the souls of men. This is an instruction of investment in the souls of men. Jesus did not leave a physical vineyard to be tended but a spiritual vineyard to be tended. Jesus did not leave a bank account to be managed as a stockbroker investing in stocks but He left His Word to be invested in the souls of men.

The faithful servants were rewarded because they invested in the few souls put in their charge. They taught them and discipled them and as a result more souls were added to the master's kingdom thus multiplying the talents. The slothful servant was judged because he did not invest in the soul put in his charge. He buried that soul, did not feed it the Gospel and therefore did not multiply on to even one other soul. Each servant was given souls in their sphere of influence to invest in using the Gospel, to teach, and to disciple.

The faithful servant's investment

Each servant, you and me, is given souls within our sphere of influence according our ability to reach, to teach, and to disciple. Some of us are given one soul, some of us two, and some of us many souls to care for. As husbands and fathers, wives and mothers, we certainly have our spouses and our children into which we must invest. As a couple we both share in the responsibility of multiplication through our children's souls. Beyond that we have neighbors, co-workers, and friends. We should note that each one of us, who has the Gospel of Christ, has been given souls or talents within our sphere of influence to reach according to our ability. Will we be faithful? The Lord will take an account when He returns.

So what was the investment that the faithful servants made with their talents? Their response was very simple "'Lord, you delivered to me five talents; look, I have gained five more talents besides them" and "Master, your mina has earned ten minas". Notice that it was the mina that earned ten more minas. This makes me think of a well discipled soul that touches other souls in his sphere of influence so that they bring more souls to the master.

What did the servants do with the talents/minas? In economic terms they traded with them: *"Then he who had received the five talents went and <u>traded with them</u>, and made another five talents"* (Matt 25:16), *"And so it was that when he returned, having received the kingdom, he then commanded these servants, to whom he had given the money, to be called to him, that he might know how much every man had <u>gained by trading</u>"* (Luke 19:15).

If this is about souls then how does one trade with souls to multiply souls? Can one soul begat another soul into the kingdom? The answer is yes: *2 Tim 2:2 And the things that you have heard from me among many witnesses, commit these to faithful men who will be able to teach others also.* You invest in the current souls in your sphere, teaching them and discipling them in the word of God, in the knowledge of His kingdom, so they may go out and teach others also.

This is not a casual event. It requires persistent endurance and immersion into the task. Have you ever known a good stock market trader or a merchant? He is watchful to what is happening to stocks in his portfolio or in the goods he trades with. He is ever awake to other buying opportunities in which that which he has can be used to purchase more. He is aware of where the growth activity is taking place. A good trader lives and breathes the market.

The investor in a few faithful men lives by the same passion. He immerses himself in understanding the Word of God. He seeks for that good soil in a soul that will be faithful to multiply. He walks with that disciple continuously to bring that disciple up to the fullness of the understanding of the master, Jesus Christ.

The objective is to multiply souls into the kingdom of heaven by investing in and with the souls currently belonging to the master such that they may multiply into adding more souls upon his return. It means a focus on discipling our spouses and children. It means being ever watchful for the opportunities in our daily contact, and being ever watchful for opportunities to reach the unreached all around the world. It means discipling our neighbors and coworkers in our sphere of influence. It means discipling an individual to knowing the fullness of the Gospel of

Christ that he may multiply in knowing the King and preaching the Gospel of the kingdom of God.

Notice that the accounting from the master takes place when the master returns having received the kingdom (Luke 19:15). This is at the end of the church age according to the timeline in section 3.3 when is the kingdom. It is the Bema seat judgement for the followers of Jesus where an accounting will be taken for what they had done with the souls put in their charge.

The slothful servant's failure

The slothful servant gives his excuse that he was afraid and so he hid the one talent he had been given. It may be that the slothful servant was not as afraid of his master while the master was in a far country as he was about criticism of his peers. In terms of investing in souls he was probably more likely timid and fearful of letting those around him know he was a servant of the Lord. **By his silence he failed to invest in the talent given to him to care for**. Maybe it was his wife or his child but he failed to tell them about Christ for fear. He valued what other men thought of him over his master's judgement. He valued what other men thought of him over the talent or soul in his charge. Maybe it was just laziness, or maybe the cares of this world distracted him so he never prayed with, studied with, or discussed the Word with the soul in his charge.

Yet the master cares for the talent or soul that is not being cared for by the slothful servant. The master takes the talent away from the slothful servant and puts it in the charge of a faithful servant who has shown he will invest in all the souls in his charge. Maybe the soul once under the care of the slothful servant is placed in the care of a Sunday school teacher when the father of the child fails to invest.

How many times have we hidden our Christianity for fear of peer criticism? How many times have we stopped telling the Gospel because of fear of being tagged offensive, intolerant, or a Bible thumper? How many times have we decided we were too tired, would rather rest, or found it inconvenient to spread the Gospel? How many moments have we lost in investing in our wives, our children, and other friends in our sphere of influence? How often have we been timid in conversing with the person sitting on the bus or airplane in the seat next to us?

How do we relate to the judgments?

The faithful servants in effect received three rewards: 1) the approval of the master "well done, good and faithful servant, 2) you were faithful over a few things, I will make you ruler over many things, and 3) enter into the joy of your Lord. Most Christians are seemingly pretty comfortable with waiting for the words on the other side of death *"enter into the joy of your Lord"*. We look forward to the rest and joy of Heaven escaping from the trials of this life and looking forward to the restored relationship with God. However that reward will be incomplete without the statement of well-done good and faithful servant. There is nothing more rewarding than the approval of a Father. But the faithful servants are given another reward, they are made ruler over many things (Matt 25:21). In (Luke 19:17) the one with ten minas was given authority over ten cities. The one with five minas was given authority over five cities. If investing in souls was the objective of the servant, authority over ten cities of souls indeed would be a huge reward and responsibility!

Lastly we have the judgment for the unfaithful servant. He also received three basic judgments; 1) he was judged a wicked and lazy servant, 2) he was reminded that he knew the master's work, how he reaped and gathered where he did not sow and yet did not act accordingly, and he was told that the least he could have done is deposited the money with the bankers who would have invested and multiplied the money, and 3) the talent he had was taken away and he was cast out of the masters presence, into outer darkness where he will regret his laziness forever.

None of us would like to hear the words of *"wicked and lazy servant"* not even from our earthly employers, so why are we so casual about our Heavenly Father? Notice the word *"lazy"* servant. The judgment was holy and true – the servant knew his master reaped and gathered where he had not sown, yet the servant did not act accordingly. The slothful servant was told at least he could have placed the talent in the hands of the bankers. What does that mean? In terms of souls I think of a man who does not feel qualified to invest in his children but he at least is diligent in putting them in the charge of those who are capable of teaching and discipling them. But even doing that, he would have forgotten that he was given this soul to invest in according to his ability.

There is a nagging question about this unfaithful servant's position with the master. Was he a servant that was not saved and not part of the kingdom of God? Was he caught up in the dragnet of the kingdom of God but was actually one of those bad fish to be discarded and burned at the end? How could a servant who knows and loves his Lord sincerely in his heart not care for the talents, the souls, the Lord gave him to take care of and nurture? How could a servant who knows the treasure we have in the King of kings, Jesus Christ not wish to share that treasure with others?

I think this servant never was a servant of the master in his heart. How could a true servant of the Lord place his fears of other men's opinion above serving the Lord? No I think this man is one who pretends to be a believer and is not one at all. He fits the characteristic of the goat being separated from the sheep in the text that follows the parable of the 10 talents (Matt 25:31 – 46). He fits the catch of the dragnet of the kingdom of God where the good and bad are sorted out at the end of time. He fits the illustration of the tares that are found among the wheat in the parable of the wheat and tares of the kingdom of God.

As Jesus said; "if you love me keep my commandments". I believe it will be natural for a child who loves his father to do the will of his father - out of love.

Summary

It is clear that this parable is about stewardship in the spreading of the Gospel so that some might hear, teaching those who do hear that they might grasp the full truth of the Gospel. It is about discipling faithful men who are able and willing to invest in others. This is a stewardship of souls with the objective of multiplying souls for the kingdom of heaven. The faithful servant investing in the souls of men as Christ commanded in the great commission is the place we want to be found when He comes. The talent and mina are used from the economy of men to illustrate for our understanding how a servant of the Lord multiplies what is of value, souls, in the economy of the kingdom of Heaven. Jesus Christ is the master and that which He values in the Kingdom of God is the souls of men.

Someone might say I don't know what souls have been given to me to invest in. Do you have a wife or husband? Do you have children? Do you have a father and a mother? Do you have brothers and sisters? Do you have a neighbor? Who will you meet today? Well then these souls have been given into your hand to invest in, especially your own family. The king will come and ask if you have shared Him with them and taught them the Word of God. You have been given the Word from the Father through Jesus to the disciples and from the disciples to you. We are to carry the words of the King to those we know. We are the ambassadors of the King. It is our responsibility. It is not a dependence on our pastor.

Will we hear those treasured words "Well done, good and faithful servant; you were faithful over a few things, I will make you ruler over many things. Enter into the joy of your Lord." Or, perish the thought will we hear those fearful words "you wicked and lazy servant... and cast the unprofitable servant into the outer darkness" because we failed to invest in the souls in our sphere of influence.

11   Living and Walking in the story of the King

I hope by this time you have realized that you are living in the greatest love story ever told. It is not something you must imagine. You are a participant in this story. Much more than an actor, the story involves a relationship between the King and you. You can see His work throughout all time and how this love story illuminates the love and the glory of the King to restore you to a relationship with Him. Not just a weekend get together, but a non-ending walk hand and hand, heart to heart, day by day, moment by moment, with our King. The intimacy described in the Bible is much greater even than that which we have with our spouses. His desire is to be one with us. One with us as He is one with the Father. It is His desire and His activity to reach into our hearts to show Himself to us so that it would become our desire to love Him out of our choice and love for Him because He first loved us.

He did not come as a conquering King but calls out to His church in courtship, an engagement betrothing the church for marriage. He allures His bride. A promise of marriage into oneness with Him forever. He delights in providing righteousness, justice, and lovingkindness to His bride. He gives His righteousness by His blood and cleanses her to remove all spot and wrinkle through washing of the Word. He administers justice and correction to mold His bride into perfection. All this He does in lovingkindness, with a gentle and humble heart. He has demonstrated His faithfulness throughout time and has given the seal of the Holy Spirit as a faithful promise.

*Behold, <u>I will allure her</u> … in that day," Says the L*ORD*, "That **you will call Me 'My Husband,' And no longer call Me 'My Master … I will betroth you to Me forever** … <u>I will betroth you to Me In righteousness and justice, In lovingkindness and mercy … I will betroth you to Me in faithfulness</u> … I will have mercy on her who had not obtained mercy; Then I will say to those who were not My people, 'You are My people!' And they shall say, 'You are my God!' " (Hosea 2:14–23)*

The last message Jesus gave before He went to the cross was a prayer for us.

> *(John 17:20-21)* ^{20} *"I do not pray for these alone, but also <u>for those who will believe in Me through their word;</u>* ^{21} ***that they all may be one, as You, Father, are in Me, and I in You; that they also may be one in Us****, that the world may believe that You sent Me.* ^{22} *And the glory which You gave Me I have given them, that they may be one just as We are one:* ^{23} <u>*I in them, and You in Me; that they may be made perfect in one*</u>*, and that the world may know that You have sent Me, and have loved them as You have loved Me.*
> ^{24} *"Father, I desire that they also whom You gave Me may be with Me where I am, that they may behold My glory which You have given Me; for You loved Me before the foundation of the world.*
> ^{25} *O righteous Father! The world has not known You, but I have known You; and these have known that You sent Me.* ^{26} *And I have declared to them Your name, and will declare it, <u>that the love with which You loved Me may be in them, and I in them.</u>"*

His prayer is for the complete fulfillment of the kingdom of God in us as we are made one with Him and the Father. Five things He asks of the Father;

1) That we would all be one with Jesus and the Father; the Father in Jesus, Jesus in us,
2) That we would be made perfect in that oneness,
3) That the glory the Father had given to Jesus would be given to us,
4) That we would be where Jesus is so that we could look on His glory,
5) And that the love by which the Father loved Jesus would be in us.

If the Father is in Jesus, and Jesus is in us then we like Jesus (John 5:30) will seek to do the Fathers will. If we do the Fathers will we will enter the kingdom of heaven (Matt 7:21). With the love that the Father had for Jesus in us we are able to love others with the love the Father loved Jesus. With that love in us we are able to export the fruit of the Spirit *"love, joy, peace, longsuffering, kindness, goodness, faithfulness, gentleness and self-control"* to the world.

No wonder the Apostle John writes those words of awe before the Father; ***Behold what manner of love the Father has bestowed on us, that we should be called children of God!*** (**1 John 3:1-3**).

In this greatest of love stories He;

1) Provided the payment for sin through the sacrifice of His Son. He has set us free from a debt we could not pay.
2) He promised eternal life to all those who believe on the Son of God. That whoever would accept His gift and believe in His heart that Jesus is the Son of God and confess with His mouth would be given eternal life
3) He adopted us into His family and calls us the children of God when we believe that Jesus is the Son of God. The Son who the Father sent to pay for our sins and to give us His Word.
4) He promised that we would be raised from the dead, to be with Him when He returns. Just as His Son was raised from the dead He is our resurrection and life to all who believe.
5) He asked of the Father and the Father sent us the Holy Spirit, God in the Spirit to live in us, to teach us, to comfort us while we are here in the world. Jesus did not leave us as orphans when He went to be with the Father.
6) He promised that he would prepare a mansion in the presence of the Father and would bring us to be there with Him to see His glory. Jesus said that if He goes to prepare a place for us to live with Him He certainly will come back to take us to be with Him.
7) Jesus asked the Father to keep us from the evil one, a prayer that keeps us in the Fathers hand. He will never loose us. Jesus defeated the evil one and conquered death at the cross and resurrection. The evil one has no power over the one in which the Holy Spirit, Jesus, and the Father reside. He that is in us is greater than he that is in the world.

8) Jesus asked for the Father to perfect us, to sanctify us, to set us aside for Him. He gave us the Word so that we might be sanctified by it. It is Jesus who is washing us by the Word as water. He is preparing those of the kingdom of God for perfection, no wrinkles, no blemish as His bride. He is preparing the church, the body of Christ, the place of the kingdom of God to perfection with Him in us and us in Him. One with Him.

9) **Then He asks that we would be one with Him and the Father – WOW!** The Father in Jesus and Jesus in us. As the Jesus dwells in us, as the Father dwells in Jesus, the Fathers dwells in our hearts. As Jesus was able to say I do nothing but the will of the Father we also have Him to enable us, His will to obey.

10) **AND that the love by which the Father loved Jesus would be in us, and Jesus would be in us.** The love of the 1st commandment to love the Father with all our heart, soul, and mind is completed with the love of the Father in Jesus and the love of Jesus in us. That love of the Father gives us the power to love our neighbor from the pure love by which He first loved us. God is love and when He is in us we love others (1 John 4:7-11).

The greatest love story ever told.

Salvation is the beginning.

The end goal He has set is oneness with Him and the Father